China in the Tokugawa World

THE EDWIN O. REISCHAUER LECTURES, 1988

Sponsored by the Dillon Fund

D1563110

China *in the* Tokugawa World

Marius B. Jansen

HARVARD UNIVERSITY PRESS

CAMBRIDGE, MASSACHUSETTS

LONDON, ENGLAND

Copyright © 1992 by the President and Fellows of
Harvard College
All rights reserved
Printed in the United States of America
Second printing, 2000

First Harvard University Press paperback edition, 2000

Library of Congress Cataloging-in-Publication Data

Jansen, Marius B.
    China in the Tokugawa World / Marius B. Jansen.
        p.   cm.
    "The Edwin O. Reischauer lectures"; 1988
    Includes bibliographical references and index.
    ISBN 0-674-11753-0 (cloth)
    ISBN 0-674-00266-0 (pbk.)
    1. Japan—Relations—China. 2. China—Relations—
    Japan.   3. Japan—History—Tokugawa period,
    1600–1868. I. Title.
DS849.C6J26   1992
303.48′252051—dc20
91-43906

to the memory of
Edwin Oldfather Reischauer (1910–1990)
and
John King Fairbank (1907–1991)

Preface

THIS BOOK began as the Edwin O. Reischauer Lectures on East Asian Affairs at the John King Fairbank Center for East Asian Research, Harvard University, in March 1988. As conceived by Roderick MacFarquhar, professor of government and director of the Fairbank Center, the Reischauer lectures are designed to restore the sense of an East Asian civilization that once pervaded all our work but has been greatly weakened by the more recent specialization on single-country histories. That specialization is the natural and inevitable product of the growth of knowledge as studies of China, Japan, Korea, and Vietnam have gained in number and in scholarly depth. Yet a great deal of the interconnectedness that used to characterize our teaching and writing has been lost. This is especially so in the study of Japan, a civilization that, for all its particularity, has been closely linked to China and a country whose men of letters prided themselves on their full participation in the cultural milieu of the continental mainland. It is also unfortunate that studies of the centuries of Tokugawa rule have suffered from excessive focus on the attenuation of Japan's ties with the West at cost to examination of relations with China.

Connected as they are with the names of Fairbank and Reischauer, these lectures have also provided me with a welcome opportunity to salute two remarkable scholars who had much to do with the direction of my own study of East Asian history. That specialization began in the early fall of 1943. Fresh from infantry basic training in Georgia and bedraggled after a long ride to Cambridge in an old Pennsylvania Railroad coach, at Harvard I was given the choice of studying Japanese or Chinese in one of the specialized training programs that the United States army had established on college campuses to prepare interpreters for the needs of the postwar world. I chose Japanese without much thought or preparation—it was, after all, the language of the country with which we were at war. I have never regretted that choice. For one thing, my future colleague Frederick W. Mote was across the courtyard in Leverett House with the Chinese contingent, and we would never have spent these decades at the same institution if we had the same specialization. More important, though, is the fact that, beginning with army and early occupation duty and extending through more than thirty visits in the years that followed, I had access to Japan and its scholars in a way that was not available to my colleagues in Chinese history. In addition, my interest in Sino-Japanese relations gave me the opportunity to interact with two communities of Japanese scholars, the sinologues as well as the specialists in Japanese history. These are surprisingly discrete communities in Japanese universities, since East Asian (Tōyōshi) and national (Kokushi) history are taught in separate departments. Over the years a deepening of knowledge has gone in tandem with a deepening of personal friendships to make my studies especially rewarding.

In the Harvard–army language program, instruction was led by a genial professor, Serge Elisséeff. The indignity of an 8:00 A.M. class five days a week represented for him a sacrifice that was, I think, an element in the friendship that followed; I am sure it was an element in his continued, close interest in my later graduate work and career, an interest that lasted until his death in Paris in 1975. Much of the hands-on language training, however, was designed by Makoto Matsukata, younger brother of Haru Matsukata Reischauer. A young man of keen intelligence and commanding presence, he later joined the American army and was serving as a member of the government section of SCAP when I returned to Japan in the fall of 1951. Later he became a businessman in Tokyo, and our paths crossed a number of times before his untimely death. Like John Fairbank, Edwin Reischauer was on government service at that time, teaching and organizing an intelligence unit many of whose members followed him to Harvard and university positions after the war.

My first meeting with John Fairbank came when I returned to Harvard in the fall of 1946. He immediately enrolled me in the first section of the Regional Studies Seminar on China he was organizing, fully aware that my principal language would continue to be Japanese. Then and thereafter, he never lost an opportunity to drive home the intellectual importance of studying China through Japan. Soon the fortunate discovery of Japanese sources of importance for the life of Sun Yat-sen and the Chinese revolution of 1911 provided a happy combination of East Asian concerns for me. This mix was very much to the taste of Edwin Reischauer when he too returned to Harvard. Japanese history and literature were still taught in alternate years by Elisséeff, but Reischauer directed the work in Japanese language and taught early Chinese history with the rigor and enthusiasm that characterized all of his work. In those years he was completing his study of Ennin's pilgrimage to China, while also developing the approaches to Japanese history and national character he first articulated in *Japan Past and Present* and *The United States and Japan*. Fairbank, in turn, was working on the first edition of *The United States and China*. It was a setting that provided hours and days of profitable discussion and debate; daily exchanges with people who were to become life-long friends and colleagues—Benjamin I. Schwartz, John W. Hall, Donald H. Shively, Howard S. Hibbett, Joseph Levenson, and many more—made those years memorable. We sometimes wondered if there would be academic positions at the end of the road, for East Asian studies in most universities and colleges were still a future hope, but all of us were delighted to be back doing what we chose to do after years of military and wartime service. The outside world was no doubt less convinced of the wisdom of our course. I recall one occasion when a Harvard-educated lawyer, hearing what I was studying, responded incredulously, "You mean to say they're teaching that there now?"

Fortunately they were, and fortunately especially for me, since I had the opportunity to study with both Reischauer and Fairbank and then to work as their first teaching assistant in the course on East Asian civilization that became famous among undergraduates as "Rice Paddies," helping to produce the slides that concluded lectures and to prepare the syllabus handouts that became the "Harvard" text of later years.

Harvard was followed by a decade at the University of Washington, where there was the new and demanding prospect of building a series of courses in Japanese history, and adding to that a course in Sino-Japanese relations. To intellectual discovery was now added institution building with a new set of colleagues, and those twin challenges continued to occupy me in the next three decades at Princeton, where Fritz Mote and I joined with other colleagues to define the kind of work we wanted to encourage.

I give this personal history to explain the setting in which I have been able to develop my work. Country specialization is essential, but it is also important, I believe, to retain a sense of East Asian civilization in the round. In our student days this was relatively easy, for the flood of publication that now makes it difficult to follow even one culture or subfield had not yet begun. It was reasonable to expect a measure of familiarity with both China and Japan, and to grope for coverage of Korea and Southeast Asia as well. But as our fields have grown it becomes more difficult to keep up with either China or Japan in adequate detail, particularly if one has any hope of keeping the broader field of "history" or "letters" in sight.

This is why the challenge that Professor MacFarquhar and the Fairbank Center presented me was at once inviting and dismaying. The chapters that follow are about Japan and Japanese attitudes toward China, but I have tried to show how important it is to balance the integrity of China and Japan as autonomous entities with an awareness of their joint membership in the larger sphere of East Asian civilization. In addition, because so much of my work has focused on modern Sino-Japanese relations, I felt it important to examine the centuries that came before. It is an ambitious task, and no one is more aware than I of how much more there is to be done at each point.

It remains to acknowledge the stimulation of discussions that followed the presentation of these themes, a seminar in which Benjamin Schwartz, Albert Craig, Harold Bolitho, Philip Kuhn, Howard Hibbett, John Schrecker, and others suggested additional leads and approaches, and the help I received from early and careful readings by William S. Atwell, Martin Collcutt, and Leonard Blussé. It is a matter of deep regret that Edwin Reischauer and John Fairbank did not live to see this reminder of the affection and respect in which I hold their memory.

M. B. J.

Contents

Illustrations

(pages 42–51)

Map of Nagasaki, 1802. In author's possession
Print of Nagasaki by Sadahide, 1862. From *Deshima: Its
Pictorial Heritage* (Nagasaki City Council on Improved
Preservation at the Registered Historical Site of Deshima,
1987). Reproduced by permission of the publisher, Chūō
Kōron Bijutsu Shuppan
Print of Soochow, showing the Chinese influence. From *Edo
jidai zushi* (Tokyo: Chikuma Shobō, 1976)
Votive painting of Suminokura ship, 1634
A Nanking ship. Courtesy of Ōba Osamu
A Ningpo ship. Courtesy of Ōba Osamu
Scroll painting of Nagasaki ship procession, 1740. From
Gairai bunka to Kyūshū (Tokyo: Heibonsha, 1973); orig-
inal scroll in Mito Shōkan
Kōfukuji Temple, Nagasaki. From Nakamura Akio and Na-
gashima Shōichi, *Nagasaki—Hirado* (Tokyo: Asahi,
1974). Photograph by Nakamura Akio
Scroll painting of China trade, ascribed to Hirowatari Ko-
shū. From *Edo jidai zushi*
Mampukuji Temple, near Uji

China in the Tokugawa World

I *The Contacts*

FOR MANY YEARS, discussions of the Tokugawa period (1600–1868) have emphasized the edicts of national seclusion. As our textbooks remind us, the edicts of the 1630s expelled the Iberian Catholics from Japan and limited foreign relations to highly attenuated contacts with Holland, China, and Korea. Dutch and Chinese traders were permitted to come to the Kyushu port of Nagasaki. Relations with Korea were delegated to the lord of Tsushima, who maintained a trading station at Pusan that also provided a channel for diplomatic communications upon the accession of a new shogun. A total of twelve Korean missions were sent to Japan during the Tokugawa years. Although negotiations were conducted on a basis of near equality, neither party was satisfied; Arai Hakuseki's efforts in the early eighteenth century to reform the ritual of the system to Japan's advantage are well known. No Tokugawa missions were sent to Korea. In the final years of the shogunate, Tokugawa bakufu negotiators attempted to place relations with Korea on a basis of interstate equality, but without success. That attempt foreshadowed the contentious relations of the early Meiji era, when Japan and Korea came to the brink of war.

Relations with China were even less formal. The bakufu, after considering the possibility of formal relations, concluded that the cost—acceptance of a tributary role in China's East Asian order—was incompatible with its dignity and with Japanese sovereignty. Chinese trading junks were permitted to come to Nagasaki from south Chinese and Southeast Asian ports, but that contact was unofficial and never on a country-to-country basis. No Chinese missions came to Japan, nor did Japan send missions to the continent. On the contrary: the Japanese warned that Chinese officials were not to accompany the trading ships. In addition to this, a separate avenue of access to Chinese goods existed for a time after the Satsuma seizure of Okinawa in 1609. Satsuma was able to profit from the Ryūkyū membership in the Chinese world order, while ceremonial visits to Japan by Ryūkyūan representatives provided further evidence for Japanese of their nation's position at the center of a separate international sphere. Thus limited, Japan's insular isolation became conspicuous in the nineteenth century with the approaches from the West, especially since it seemed so much in contrast with the relative openness shown in its sixteenth-century response to Western trade and religion. It became the most remarked-upon aspect of the Tokugawa system.

This remained so because Japan's modern historical tradition was heavily affected by the work and thought of Leopold von Ranke, whose disciple Ludwig Riess taught world history at the Imperial University in Tokyo from 1887 to 1902, helping to convince the academy of the primacy of foreign policy in the creation of all modern states.[1] From Western and Rankean perspectives, foreign relations—or the lack of them—were central to the emergence of a modern Japanese state.

More recent scholarship, however, conditions this view by

1. Leonard Blussé, "Japanese Historiography and European Sources," in P. C. Emmer and H. L. Wesseling, eds., *Reappraisals in Overseas History* (Leiden: Leiden University Press, 1979).

stressing ways in which Japan's isolation was also part of a Japan-centered world order. Bob T. Wakabayashi reminds us that the forms of seclusion changed over time and did not in fact become pillars of Tokugawa ideology until the nineteenth century, when bakufu authorities began to refer to isolation as a cardinal aspect of the legacy of Ieyasu's rule.[2] Ronald P. Toby was early to point out that the term *sakoku* (closed country) first appeared in a translation of Kaempfer's account of his stay in Japan, and that it had meaning chiefly with respect to Japan's relations with the West and not to those with its neighbors in East Asia.[3] Tashiro Kazui has demonstrated the importance of Japan's relations with Korea—imports via Tsushima sometimes exceeded those to Nagasaki; they were considered so important that the bakufu exempted the Korea trade from its prohibitions on the export of silver, even after a shortage of bullion had led to a reminting of coinage within Japan.[4] The work of Ōba Osamu has contributed immensely to our knowledge of cultural interchange between Japan and China.[5] In addition, our increased awareness of the intellectual vitality of late Tokugawa Japan has demonstrated that the country was in some sense open intellectually before it was opened diplomatically and commercially. As a result, *sakoku* begins to seem more symbol than fact. It can also be argued that China was no less "closed," and Korea more so, than Japan; each country tolerated trade only through highly

2. *Anti-Foreignism and Western Learning: The New Theses of 1825* (Cambridge: Harvard University Press, 1986).

3. *State and Diplomacy in Early Modern Japan: Asia in the Development of the Tokugawa Bakufu* (Princeton: Princeton University Press, 1984) and "Reopening the Question of *Sakoku:* Diplomacy in the Legitimation of the Tokugawa Bakufu," *Journal of Japanese Studies* 3:2 (Summer 1977).

4. *Kinsei Ni-Chō tsūkō-bōekishi no kenkyū* (Tokyo, 1981) and "Foreign Relations During the Edo Period: *Sakoku* Reexamined," *Journal of Japanese Studies* 8:2 (Summer 1982).

5. *Edo jidai in okeru Chūgoku bunka juyō no kenkyū* (Tokyo 1984), and other works cited below.

structured institutional forms, and certainly neither China
nor Korea experienced anything like the intellectual stimulus
that Japanese scholars derived from outside, especially Western, learning.

The image of an isolated Japan whose inhabitants were cut
off from the outside world also conflicts with a second image
we have of Tokugawa culture: a civilization oriented more
than ever before toward the language and classical culture of
continental China. It has long been accepted that Chinese influence rose to a peak in the Tokugawa years. The rising tide
of literacy meant that more Japanese could read and write
Chinese. The production of poetry in Chinese, something expected of every educated person, was so great that it may have
exceeded the amount of verse composed in Japanese.[6] It can
of course be argued that Japanese writers who were expressing themselves in Chinese were not conscious of any national
distinctions as they did so. But by the eighteenth century there
are many indications that this did in fact pose psychological
problems. Yamazaki Ansai's disciples asked him about their
duty in the event of a Chinese invasion led by Confucius, the
sage they had been taught to venerate. Certainly the irritation
displayed by Japanese nativist scholars at the sinocentric be-
havior of their Confucian contemporaries put the two tradi-
tions into sharp contrast. Other monuments of popular culture, like the stage treatment of Koxinga, show the same
thing. So questions about the way Tokugawa Japanese
thought about China are important. It is necessary to begin
with consideration of the contacts that took place in the Kyushu port of Nagasaki.

6. Yaichi Haga, "Literature of the Meiji Era," in Shigenobu Okuma, ed., *Fifty Years of New Japan*, vol. 2 (London, 1909), asserts that to overlook the production of books in Chinese in Edo Japan would be "to miss the greater and perhaps the better half . . . since so far as quantity is concerned the former are twice as numerous as the latter" (p. 424).

The Nagasaki Setting

In late Muromachi and sixteenth-century years, intermittent trade and piracy resulted in large-scale contact between Japan and China along coastal points from Kyushu to the Wakayama peninsula. During the period of earlier Muromachi stability under Ashikaga Yoshimitsu (shogun 1368–1394), a tally system imposed by the Ming emperors restricted Japanese trade to ships authorized for travel by the Muromachi bakufu. But by the late sixteenth century the devolution of power in both Japan and China led to the emergence of semi-private fleets that brought tumult and disorder to East Asian coasts. In Japan, pirate bands known to history as *wakō* gathered along the Kyushu coast and recruited Korean, Chinese, and Japanese adventures who disrupted life along the southern Korean and Chinese littoral for many decades. With the decline of central power on both sides of the East China Sea, private fleets in south China held out against the late Ming and early Ch'ing forces throughout much of the seventeenth century. The fact and memory of wakō depredation, added to the ruinous invasions of Korea by Hideyoshi's vassals in 1592 and 1597, made it unlikely that Japanese relations with the continental powers of Korea and China would proceed smoothly in the early Tokugawa years.

The weakness of central power and public order, and the high degree of commercial and military vigor of the warrior society of western Japan, made the island of Kyushu and its environs a good base from which Japanese buccaneers, Chinese expatriates, and Korean renegades could produce a last flurry of wakō piracy in the sixteenth century. The Korean court responded to the incursions of robber bands, first by military efforts that were only rarely successful and then by trying to coopt Japanese coastal barons, particularly the Sō house of Tsushima, into its official system with privileges of trade, promises of monopoly, and rewards of official appointment. This was the origin of the Tsushima trading station at Pusan. At one time there were two more such stations, at modern Chinhae and Ulsan.[7] Ming authorities were more successful with punitive naval expeditions against the pirates, but their problems were magnified by the simultaneous need to engage in land warfare to protect the northern border against the Mongols and Manchus.[8] In 1557 and 1567 Korea worked out arrangements with Tsushima that permitted the Sō daimyo of that domain to send thirty vessels a year to trade; thereafter Korea was no longer troubled by pirates. China, however, remained an inviting target.

Between 1440 and 1550, Chinese sources reported twenty-five wakō raids, but "they mentioned no fewer than 467 separate incidents in the single decade between 1551 and 1560 and added another 75 for the ten years from 1561 to 1570, when the tide began to ebb."[9] The new wave of brigandage, emanating from Kyushu, was sometimes Chinese in leadership. Wang Chih, a native of Anhwei, first came to Japan in the 1540s and established himself at Hirado, where he received shelter from (and contributed to the wealth of) the Matsuura lord. In time he became the leader of a pirate band of several thousand men. Links to other pirate bands from the China coast and the Chusan Islands produced formidable groups of freebooters, who recruited followers from the southern islands of Japan. The same pattern reappeared with the late Ming leader Cheng Chih-lung and his son Cheng

7. Jurgis Elisonas (George Elison), "Japan's Relations with China and Korea," chap. 6 in *Cambridge History of Japan*, vol. 4, *Early Modern Japan* (Cambridge: Cambridge University Press, 1991), provides a splendid account of pirate depredations and activities in the context of Kyushu political history.

8. Arthur Waldron, *The Great Wall of China: From History to Myth* (Cambridge: Cambridge University Press, 1990), provides a skillful account of Ming defense problems.

9. Elisonas, pp. 249–250.

Ch'eng-kung, the famous Koxinga of the seventeenth century. A work entitled *Jih-pen i-chien* (c. 1564) by Chen Shun-kung, which is the chief contemporary source for description of wakō depredations, begins with the due resentment of the Chinese drifters and exiles who led or guided many of the numerous raids on the China coast, but goes on to point out that "from Kii, on these barbarians' eastern seacoast, to the south and west, through the San'yō and the San'in regions to Wakasa and the barbarians' west, there is no place where the people have not been incited to join in the raids. They may call themselves merchants, but are in actuality brigands." [10]

It should be noted from the dating of these events that, in Elisonas' words, "Both the merchants and the missionaries [from the West] were carried to Japan in the backwash of the *wakō* trade." [11] Even so, there is reason to share in his astonishment that the so-called Confucian scholar Yu-feng, who acted as interpreter for the Portuguese on Tanegashima, where the Japanese made their historic acquaintance with the arquebus, was in actuality the same pirate trader Wang Chih who had earlier sailed from Hirado. [12]

These events had as corollary the diffusion of Chinese along the Japanese littoral from the Kii peninsula to southern Kyushu. There were "Chinatowns" of varying size along the coast everywhere in Kyushu and also in Yamaguchi, Matsuyama, and as far east as Kawagoe and Odawara in the Kantō. Nobunaga invited Chinese artisans to create the tiles for his castle at Azuchi, and those skills soon spread to all parts of Japan. Chinese artisans were also recruited by Ieyasu and other warrior lords, and some were enfeoffed with significant

---

10. Quoted in ibid., pp. 254–255.

11. Elisonas, "Christianity and the Daimyo," chap. 7 in *Cambridge History of Japan*, vol. 4, p. 303.

12. Tanaka Takeo, "Chūsei no Kyūshū to tairiku," in Fukuoka UNESCO, ed., *Gairai bunka to Kyūshū* (Tokyo, 1973), pp. 97ff.

land and residences.[13] English and Dutch visitors who wrote from Japan frequently spoke of the presence of well-rewarded and highly regarded Chinese master artisans. As order improved in Japan and declined in China in the early years of the seventeenth century, many of these artisans chose to remain in Japan, changing their names and consequently disappearing from the registers of resident Chinese. This was true not only at the center but also in Kyushu provinces such as Hyūga, Satsuma, and Ōsumi. Undoubtedly many such craftsmen disappeared into Japanese society in the early decades of the Tokugawa period.

When Japanese trade with the West began in the sixteenth century, Nagasaki was a small fishing village. Portuguese ships began to call there in 1571, and in 1580 the local lord, Ōmura Sumitada, desperate for help against his stronger neighbors, donated the city to the Jesuits as their headquarters.[14] With Hideyoshi's conquest of Kyushu in 1587, that donation was voided, and from then on the city, now a growing port town, was under central control. Hideyoshi appointed Nabeshima Naoshige of Saga as his deputy, or *daikan,* and when Nabeshima joined in the Korean campaign of 1592 the Karatsu lord took his place with the title of *bugyō* (magistrate). Local administration for a time was entrusted to a Christian townsman, Murayama Tōan, who was appointed daikan and who served until his execution in 1619 because of his faith. Daikan continued to be appointed until 1676, after which local affairs were in the hands of town elders (*machi toshiyori*). The Edo bakufu continued to entrust local matters

13. Nakamura Tadashi, "Kinsei no Nihon kakyō," ibid., p. 136.
14. George Elison, in *Deus Destroyed: The Image of Christianity in Early Modern Japan* (Cambridge: Harvard University Press, 1973), documents the "Donation of Don Bartholomeu," pp. 94–95. See also Diego Pacheco, "The Founding of the Port of Nagasaki and Its Cession to the Society of Jesus," *Monumenta Nipponica* 25:3–4 (1970), 303–323.

to residents, but exerted overall control through the appointment of bugyō from among Tokugawa retainers; they were normally drawn from the *hatamoto* (bannermen) ranks and reported directly to Edo. There were normally two bugyō, one resident in Edo and the other on duty in Nagasaki. They alternated position in the autumn.

Once the Tokugawa bakufu decided to put foreign trade under its own direction at Nagasaki, the city and its administration began to grow. Long before the formalization of requirements under Iemitsu in the 1630s, Tokugawa Ieyasu showed a determination to center foreign trade at Nagasaki. In plans (which proved abortive) for a resumption of tally trade with Ming China, he directed that from 1616 on Chinese ships should trade only at Nagasaki, regardless of which port they entered. That year Shimazu Iehisa of Satsuma, anxious to demonstrate his loyalty to the bakufu, ordered that Chinese ships coming to southern Kyushu be sent on to Nagasaki. Other Kyushu daimyo were quick to show themselves equally loyal, as when Katō Kiyomasa sent eighty-seven hostages who had been seized in the Korean campaign back to Fukien for repatriation.[15]

As trade became concentrated in Nagasaki, most overseas Chinese found it necessary to head there as well, although some chose to return to China instead. Nagasaki soon came to have the largest number of overseas Chinese in Japan. Iwao Seiichi quotes one Chinese writer to the effect that the number of Chinese there grew from twenty to over two thousand between 1608 and 1618.[16] Chinese lived in all parts of Nagasaki

---

15. Nakamura, "Kinsei no Nihon kakyō," p. 154.

16. Iwao Seiichi, "Japanese Foreign Trade in the 16th and 17th Centuries," *Acta Asiatica* 30 (Tokyo, 1976), 11; see also Aloysius Chang, "The Chinese Community of Nagasaki in the First Century of the Tokugawa Period, 1603–1688," doctoral dissertation (St. John's University, 1970).

until the special Chinese quarter, the *Tōjin yashiki,* was constructed at the end of the century. They made it the most cosmopolitan city in Japan.

One aspect of this was the development of temples for the Chinese residents. Three such were established before the sakoku decrees, one to provide for the needs of provincials from the Chekiang, Kiangsu, and Kiangsi ("Nanking") areas and two for Fukien, Foochow, and Changchow-Ch'uanchow. They were popularly known as the Nanking, Changchow, and Foochow temples. Established in 1623, 1628, and 1629 respectively, they began as informal activities of merchant leaders and went on to invite formal incorporation by priests from the mainland who conducted proper dedication services a few years later. Nominally Buddhist, they focused particular attention on the popular goddess Matsu, the guardian patron of sea voyagers. Of these temples the first, which became the avenue for invitation of monks who went on to central Japan to found the Ōbaku temple of Mampukuji at Uji later in the seventeenth century, had a cultural importance that extended far beyond Nagasaki. A fourth Chinese temple, which became known as the Canton temple, was established in 1678 and reflected the rising importance in the trade of provincials from Kwangtung. These institutions surely played an important role in the lives of expatriate Chinese sailors and merchants thrown upon their own resources far from home, and they figured in Nagasaki cultural and commercial life in many ways. For the bakufu they also provided a way of incorporating the resident Chinese in the system of temple registration (*shūmon aratame*).[17]

Commercial growth was accompanied by administrative expansion. Nagasaki was divided into an "inner city," itself made up of a core—the six *machi* (streets) dating from Jesuit

17. Nakamura, "Kinsei no Nihon kakyō," pp. 233–271.

days, ultimately twenty-three, self-governing under a *toshi-yori* (elder) and exempt from land tax—and an outer city, consisting of territory annexed as the port grew in importance. Three villages, ultimately forty-three machi, made up an "outer city," whose tax constituted stipends for the daikan and later the town elders. The tax base remained very modest; Nagasaki lived on and for foreign trade. At the end of the seventeenth century, the whole was rated at only 3,435 koku (the five-bushel unit of rice volume used for assessments). The bakufu's bugyō were in overall charge of all this, but their chief responsibility was for general administration of foreign trade and coordination of measures for defense.

Within the shogun-held (*tenryō*) area, a distinction was made between householders and renters, as was standard in towns, both for special assessments and for allocation of profits from foreign trade.[18] By the time of Genroku, at the end of the century, the two bugyō had become four, and they were ranked with those for Osaka and Kyoto. Merchants were called on to provide the costs of construction required in connection with foreign trade. They were charged for the artificial island of Deshima, originally built for the Portuguese and inherited by the Dutch, through assessments levied according to the frontage of their establishments in the inner city. In the 1690s construction of the Chinese quarter was funded in the same way. In their turn the merchants were not backward about petitioning for redress when trade went poorly or when the distribution of profits seemed unjust. The efforts of bakufu administrators to keep things reasonably equitable helps to account for changes in the way trade was managed.

The Nagasaki magistrate had under him four toshiyori for administration of the inner city. For the outer city, administration was somewhat more complex; finances were in the

18. Ibid., pp. 176ff.

hands of a daikan who reported to the finance commissioner in Edo.[19] The defense of Nagasaki was first assigned to the domain of Fukuoka as part of its military service (*gunyaku*) to the bakufu. Fukuoka began by stationing a force of a thousand men; soon it shared this burden with Saga in alternate years. In times of stress, as when the Portuguese tried to reopen relations in 1647, these numbers could be augmented by other Kyushu and Shikoku domains to reach a force of 50,000 men, and residents were levied for the costs of building a floating boom or bridge to block the harbor. Printmakers provide impressive evidence of the land and naval preparations. Thirty-six western domains maintained stations (*yashiki*) at Nagasaki.

Once the Edo system of foreign trade was worked out, the bakufu also developed ways for structured access to news of the outer world. After 1644 Dutch and Chinese ship captains were ordered to prepare *fūsetsugaki*. These reports were submitted in three copies; one went to Edo, one to the bugyō, and a third to the interpreters. Once they reached Edo, these reports were combined with those from Tsushima and Satsuma about Korea and Ryūkyū. In addition there was contact with the outer world through doctors, monks, painters, and the visits of Korean and Ryūkyūan emissaries. Publications were imported. Special news, as on the capture of the would-be missionary Sidotti in 1708 or about the alarming Western advances on Asia in later years, could produce emergency inquiries and reports.

Nagasaki was thus a city that lived on and for foreign trade. Arrangements for its administration, defense, and in-

19. Nakamura Tadashi, *Kinsei Nagasaki bōekishi no kenkyū* (Tokyo, 1988), provides the fullest exposition of the Nagasaki setting and adds a chart of administrative positions. See also Nakamura's "Nagasaki to sakoku," prepared for a 1989 symposium on Kyushu and Japanese history and forthcoming from the National University of Singapore.

telligence were all geared to this, and its culture reflected the foreign presence. The fishing village of the sixteenth century grew into an important city. Still, its position at the outermost rim of the Japanese islands ruled out the possibility of its attaining the size of the cities of central Japan. Its population was about 25,000 in 1609. It grew steadily during the seventeenth century to peak at 64,523 in the Genroku year of 1696. As trade stopped growing and then declined, the population fell with it. By 1703 it had fallen to 50,148, and in 1715, when Arai Hakuseki's additional restrictions cut trade further, it fell to 42,553.[20] The city's population thus rose and fell with the volume of shipping that entered its port. So too with its administrative structure: the four bugyō of the peak years became three again, and then two.

One wishes that there were some way of working out figures for residents of Chinese origin among these numbers. It is possible to be specific for only one occupational group, the interpreters who were incorporated into the official network to translate documents and intelligence reports, and to look into and help adjudicate the problems of the community formed by the hundreds of Chinese sailors and traders found in the city.

Interpreters were divided into two major groups, for Dutch (*Oranda tsūji*) and for Chinese (*Tō tsūji*), with additional categories for apprentices. The "Chinese" interpreters, however, were really responsible for all of Asia, with the result that nomenclature became anomalous: *Tō tsūji yaku shokoku kata* included a category for China (*Tō tsūji yaku Tō-kata*), while other Southeast Asian countries were grouped as "other" (*ikoku*).[21] In the seventeenth century those other countries for which interpreters were maintained included

---

20. Nakamura, *Kinsei Nagasaki bōekishi no kenkyū*, pp. 207–214.

21. A convenient listing and discussion of the organization of interpreters can be found in Chang, "Chinese Community," pp. 69–90.

Thailand, Vietnam, "Luzon," and India.[22] For the most part, though, ships from all these areas were sent by overseas Chinese traders resident there. The China branch of interpreters began with the appointment of a Ming Chinese named Feng Hui in 1604.

The interpreters maintained a rather familial establishment, and their students and successors were relatives. Wada Masahiko has charted the generational development of several Chinese and Vietnamese interpreters from applications, appointments, remuneration and salary changes, and naturalization. Since China became overwhelmingly the most important trading partner, China specialists were better remunerated than were those for Southeast Asia. As time went on, moreover, ships from the outer regions declined in number. This may not have been accidental. Kamiya Nobuyuki has suggested that the startling appearance of Sidotti in 1708 may well have had an effect on the reforms instituted by Arai Hakuseki seven years later. The bakufu, he believes, established a Luzon-Macao line beyond which Catholic subversion could be anticipated, and relied on those who came to Nagasaki to bring warning or advance word of more distant traders beyond that line. In addition, restrictions on trade that the Ch'ing instituted in the eighteenth century, limiting outside contacts to the port of Canton, would have made it more difficult for coastal junks from areas beyond that point to make their way to Japan.[23]

22. Iwao Seiichi, "Kinsei Nagasaki bōeki ni kansuru suryōteki kōsatsu," *Shigaku zasshi* 62 (November 1953), provides charts showing that between 1600 and 1660 about one third of the "Chinese" ships coming to Nagasaki were from Southeast Asia; in 1660–1680 only one fourth were from the China mainland.

23. "Kyūshū no kokusai kankei: sakoku to higashi Ajiya," forthcoming from the National University of Singapore. See also Wada Masahiko, "Interpreters of Vietnamese in Nagasaki under the Tokugawa Shogunate with Reference to the Importance of Chinese in Viet-Japan Economic Relations in the Late 17th Century," paper presented in 1983 and summarized in *Proceedings of the Thirty-First International*

The Cargoes

Our understanding of the larger significance of the trade in Nagasaki has undergone remarkable development in recent years. William S. Atwell's work on currency and bullion movements links Chinese and Japanese economic history to broad world trends. The vast expansion of bullion movements in both China and Japan, he finds, "helped to facilitate high levels of public expenditure, almost frenetic urban growth, and intense economic competition, all of which proved politically and socially disruptive. The late 1630s and 1640s brought unfavorable weather that led to famine and disease in both China and Japan, and the seclusion restrictions, coming at a time when the Chinese economy had become particularly dependent on Japanese silver, can have had their share in late Ming political distress." Clearly, then, a "much more intensive linking of continents and economies during the late fifteenth and early sixteenth centuries . . . marked the beginnings of what is sometimes called 'early modern history' or the 'early modern world.' " [24]

One begins with the facts of the economic expansion of Ming China. Its unsuccessful attempts to substitute paper for solid currency were abandoned in the fifteenth century. In 1436 the state permitted the commutation of tax payments in southeast China to silver, and before long the "single whip" tax reforms made this general throughout all of China. The

---

Congress of Human Sciences in Asia and North Africa, ed. Yamamoto Tatsurō (Tokyo, 1984), vol. 1, pp. 429–441.

24. "Setting the Stage: Notes on Bullion Mining, Monetary Policy, and Foreign Trade in China Before the Coming of the Portuguese," forthcoming in a conference volume, "International History of Early-Modern East Asia"; "Ming Observers of Ming Decline: Some Chinese Views on the 'Seventeenth-Century Crisis' in Comparative Perspective," *Journal of the Royal Asiatic Society* 2 (London, 1988); "Sakoku and the Fall of the Ming Dynasty," in Yamamoto, ed., *Proceedings,* pp. 438–439.

need for silver thus produced, combined with economic growth in south China and the expansion of Chinese trade in Southeast Asia, resulted in China's soaking up much of the world's available silver. The development of mines in China helped to meet some of this need, but by the sixteenth century Japanese mines were available to take up a good deal of the slack.

Kobata Atsushi has detailed the expansion of mining in Japan beginning in the 1530s, as Sengoku daimyo competed for wealth.[25] In Suruga, Noto, Sado, and Kai a combination of new mines and new technologies of extraction, probably Chinese in origin and imported through Korea, made Japan a world producer of silver for almost a century. The demand for silver in China resulted in its having a high value relative to gold, while its abundance in Japan made the exchange for gold in China attractive for traders. Asao Naohiro writes that "Japan may have accounted for as much as one third of the world's silver output at the end of the sixteenth century and beginning of the seventeenth century."[26] The extravagant splendor of Momoyama art, with its decorative use of gold, was one byproduct of the opulence enjoyed by the despots who led in the unification of Japan.

The trade that resulted was dominated by the exchange of Japanese bullion, some gold but mostly silver and later copper, for Chinese silk. Kobata states flatly that, in the seventeenth and early eighteenth centuries, Japan was the world's largest copper-producing country. The explosion of economic and military vitality in sixteenth-century Japan created a market that was not easily satisfied—nor could it be permanently

25. "The Production and Uses of Gold and Silver in Sixteenth and Seventeenth-Century Japan," trans, W. D. Burton, *Economic History Review* 2nd ser. 18 (August 1965), 245–266; *Kin-gin bōekishi no kenkyū* (Kyoto, 1976).

26. "The Sixteenth-Century Unification," chap. 2 in *Cambridge History of Japan*, vol. 4, p. 61.

sustained. Silk yarn, especially white raw silk (*shiroito*), had a ready sale in the merchant capitals and castle towns. The few Europeans who were privileged to see the castles of the unifiers give vivid descriptions of their splendor.[27] Katō Eiichi quotes a Spanish merchant who was in Japan until about 1620: "Since the Taicosama [Hideyoshi] subjugated the whole nation twenty-four years ago, the people have come to dress more luxuriously than ever, and raw silk imported from China and Manila is now not sufficient to meet the demand of the Japanese."[28] These goods were meant for the urban upper classes and the new military aristocrats. It was a large market that could absorb some 4,000 piculs a year. But imports in excess of that would, from Iwao Seiichi's figures, create an oversupply and threaten profits.

These rival forces—strong but limited demand and the desire to maintain and monopolize profits—determined the course of events that ended with the restraints on travel and trade of the Edo years. For some time, the restrictions were Chinese in origin. Ming China's experience of freebooting Japanese raiders led it to sever all relations in 1557 and to ban Chinese traders from venturing abroad. Within a decade it relaxed the ban in response to pleas from south China to permit Chinese ships to visit Southeast Asian ports—but the prohibitions on visiting Japan were maintained. Permits for trips to Southeast Asia began with fifty, but within a few short years they were two and three times that number. Hideyoshi's

27. Michael Cooper, ed., *They Came to Japan: An Anthology of European Reports on Japan, 1543–1640* (Berkeley: University of California Press, 1965). Luis Frois, S. J., on Gifu: "I wish I were a skilled architect or had the gift of describing places well, because I sincerely assure you that of all the palaces and houses I have seen in Portugal, India, and Japan, there has been nothing to compare with this as regards luxury, wealth and cleanliness" (p. 131); and on Azuchi, "the uppermost [story] is entirely gilded" (p. 134).

28. "The Japan-Dutch Trade in the Formative Period of the Seclusion Policy—Particularly on the Raw Silk Trade by the Dutch Factory at Hirado, 1620–1640," *Acta Asiatica* 30 (Tokyo, 1976), 45.

invasions of Korea, drawing him into conflict with Ming armies in the 1590s, made it all the more certain that direct contact with Japan would remain illegal.

For Japanese consumers, the return of Chinese traders to Southeast Asia provided renewed access to Chinese goods. The result was a carrying trade in which the competition was between Japanese (merchant and daimyo) ships and European, first Portuguese and then Dutch, shipping. Soon after he completed the unification of Japan, Hideyoshi began issuing permits for foreign trade. His system had some precedents from Muromachi days, but with unification it became far more systematic and effective. Hideyoshi dominated the market, and he let others purchase silk only after he met his own needs.

Tokugawa Ieyasu continued these measures in the years after his victory at Sekigahara. In 1603 he named Ogasawara Tamemune, a trusted vassal, as Nagasaki bugyō. The next year he ordered the leading merchants of Kyoto, Sakai, and Nagasaki to form a thread guild, the *itowappu*. A few years later Osaka and Edo merchants were permitted to join. The guild's name is written with characters that indicate its function: allocating the products of foreign trade.

Next came early steps to control foreign trade through the requirement of permits for overseas voyages. Under Ieyasu these were frequently extended to foreign merchants and ships, many of them Chinese. But those in turn were frequently used as a cover for high bakufu officials who were trading illegally.[29] In the early 1630s the original permit, the *shuin-jō*, had to be supplemented by a second, known as a

29. Nagazumi Yōko, "Japan's Isolationist Policy as Seen Through Dutch Source Materials," *Acta Asiatica* 22 (1972), quotes a 1641 letter by the Hirado factory head: "Many other junks set sail also under a Chinese name. In actuality, however, these junks belong to high officials who pursue their personal profit. Now that the trade license of the Shogunate has not yet been issued, the prices of the imported goods are exorbitant" (p.20).

hoshō. Next these were limited to seven families or individuals. One so favored, interestingly enough, was the son of the English pilot Will Adams, who continued to use his father's title, Miura Anjin. Before this *shuin-sen* system was discontinued in 1635, a total of 350 permits had been issued. Of these 43 were granted to Chinese and 38 to European applicants.[30]

It is probable that the crews of even the Japanese-licensed ships included non-Japanese, but if one assumes for each of the 259 Japanese-sponsored ships an average crew of 225 (ships could carry from 400 to 650 men), then over 58,000 Japanese journeyed overseas in a little more than three decades. Add to this the tide of Japanese adventurers, most of whom ended as expatriates in the Japan-towns of Southeast Asia, and one has some idea of a trend that, had it been permitted to continue, might have been very significant for later Japanese and world history.

Carl Steenstrup, by way of comparison, comes to the following figures for North Sea coastal societies: between 1600 and 1700, 324,000 people left Holland for Asia on 1,768 ships. During the next century, another 671,000 followed on 2,930 ships. He assumes that one third of these people returned to Europe. Now if one hypothesizes a continuation to 1800 of the early seventeenth-century rate of Japanese shuin-sen travel, some 800,000 Japanese, voyaging on several thousand ships, might have made overseas journeys to Southeast Asia. The figures, in other words, would have been broadly comparable to those for northern Europe, although the Japanese passengers would have been drawn from a larger population. Had that been the case, it can be argued, Japanese so-

---

30. For a discussion of the shuin-sen system in English, see Robert LeRoy Innes, "The Door Ajar: Japan's Foreign Trade in the Seventeenth Century," dissertation (University of Michigan, 1980), pp. 106ff. The classic study is Iwao Seiichi, *Shuinsen bōekishi no kenkyū* (rev. ed., Tokyo, 1985).

ciety would surely have been quite different and considerably more international in nature. However contrary to fact, these calculations bring home the extent of external trade and travel in the early decades of the Edo period.[31]

What matters, however, is the clear evidence that trade was to a good degree international on both sides of the world. Will Adams arrived in Japan as the pilot of a Dutch ship. Crews were made up of adventurers and daredevils as well as misfits, and there was a good deal of recruitment at all ports to replace deserters. East India Company (VOC) employees included Kaempfer, Thunberg, von Siebold, and many other non-Dutch. The "Japanese" pirates in their turn had come from many nations, and it is probably wrong to think that they thought of themselves as particularly Japanese, or even that very many people did at that point. So too with the men who came crowding into Nagasaki harbor in junks; they were predominantly Chinese, but they hailed from Tongking, Siam, and Malay points of origin as well as the Fukien coast. The Nagasaki interpreters included people competent in Siamese and Vietnamese, and during the early years Portuguese was the lingua franca there and at Batavia.[32]

At any rate, Tokugawa trade grew to significant proportions. Japanese ships carried silver, copper, iron, sulfur, camphor and rice, and paid, principally in precious metals, for cotton fabrics, deerskins and sharkskins for sword hilts, gunpowder for bullets, sugar and other foodstuffs, but especially

31. These calculations are not without challenge. Steenstrup provides them in "Scandinavians in Asian Waters in the 17th Century: On the Sources for the History of the Participation of Scandinavians in Early Dutch Ventures into Asia", *Acta Orientalia* 43 (1982), 69–83, and bases them on figures provided by J. R. Bruijn, F. S. Gaastra, and I. Schöffer, *Dutch Asiatic Shipping in the 17th and 18th Centuries* (The Hague, 1987). But this source points out that "until around 1680 generally nearly half the ships stayed in Asia, from then on this became generally less." For this and other qualifications, see pp. 143–157.

32. Leonard Blussé, *Strange Company: Chinese Settlers, Mestizo Women and the Dutch in VOC Batavia* (Dordrecht: Foris, 1986), p. 165.

for silk. Japanese traders came so well supplied with silver for their purchases that even the dominant Spanish sometimes had trouble acquiring their quota of goods in Manila. Deer-skins imported to Japan reached 250,000 in some years, with the result that certain kinds of deer became almost extinct in Luzon; alternate sources of supply in Siam also dried up. All of this provided a handsome profit for the bakufu, one that could be maintained as long as Japanese mines continued to produce at a high level. Iwao Seiichi points out that "the amount of Japanese silver poured into foreign trade in the heyday of Japan's overseas trade, 1615 to 1625, reached a tremendous value, roughly estimated at 130,000–160,000 kilograms, equal to 30 or 43 percent of the total world silver production outside Japan. This explains why European and Asian merchants were so enthusiastic about developing trade with Japan." [33]

The familiar story of the institution of the exclusion policy thus begins to look different when it is considered in terms of Japan's Asian trade instead of in the context of fear of Christianity. There was that too, of course, and the Shimabara rebellion served to convince the most reluctant bakufu officials of the nature of the problem. But that does not allow for Ieyasu's keen interest in foreign trade, or the fact that Christianity was largely snuffed out before the exclusion edicts, or especially the fact that constraints on Asian and Chinese trade had no explicit relation to the anti-Christian measures. The principal considerations were those of order and hierarchy, which are to be related to the institutional history of the Tokugawa system.

In Ieyasu's time *shuin-jō* were accessible to some daimyo, to private individuals and houses, and to temples. The daimyo were the first to be frozen out, though the famous

---

33. "Japanese Foreign Trade," *Acta Asiatica*, p. 10

Date mission to Spain came as late as 1613. The *hoshō,* or guarantee, system inaugurated in 1631 tightened the reins: a shipowner now needed specific authorization from the rōjū, extended by the Nagasaki bugyō, to leave the country. As noted, these permits were restricted to a select group of seven families or individuals, each with a special and particular tie to the Tokugawa. One of the most interesting of these, Suminokura Ryōi, was the son of a Saga pawnbroker whose father had traveled to China to study medicine. The son married the daughter of a Kyoto moneylender with powerful connections, including a tie to Itakura Katsushige, the bakufu representative in Kyoto. Suminokura's informal assignments included negotiations with the rulers of the Trinh domain in North Vietnam, and for the preparation of diplomatic documents he was able to call on the services of the Confucian scholar Fujiwara Seika—indeed, he seems to be the one who introduced Hayashi Razan, Ieyasu's counselor, to Seika. With contacts of this order, Suminokura qualified for his permit.[34]

The institutionalization of authority in the next Tokugawa generation eliminated freewheeling of this sort. Ieyasu's relatively relaxed way of dealing with the people he found interesting, including foreigners like Will Adams, was not continued by his son Hidetada. Under Iemitsu, the third shogun, structure and order replaced informality and confidence. To this one must add the influence of the Dutch, who did all they could to encourage the exclusion of their rivals by encouraging the Japanese in their paranoia about Catholicism and by assuring the Japanese that they could provide for their trading needs. The Japanese were absolutely right about the Jesuits, Maurice of Nassau assured the bakufu in a communication of 1610: "the Society of Jesus, under cover of the sanctity of

34. Hayashiya Tatsusaburō, *Suminokura Saian* (Ryōi) (Tokyo, 1978); I owe this reference to Martin Collcutt. See also Innes, "The Door Ajar," pp. 138ff, and Kawashima Motojirō, *Tokugawa shoki no kaigai bōekika* (Osaka, 1916).

religion, intends to convert the Japanese to its religion, gradually to split the excellent kingdom of Japan, and further to lead the country to civil war."[35] A decade later the Dutch warned that, so long as the bakufu permitted Japanese ships to visit foreign ports, it would be impossible to be sure that Catholic missionaries were not being smuggled into Japan. To substantiate this, they identified two missionaries who had returned from Manila on a Japanese ship in 1620 by disguising themselves as merchants.

With the events of the next decade—the ban on overseas travel by Japanese in 1633, the Shimabara rebellion in 1637, and full implementation of the seclusion system with the decrees of 1639—the Dutch had their way. The profits that resulted were probably worth the indignity of their removal to Nagasaki from Hirado in 1641. What they did not count on was that Nagasaki and its guild merchants, with whom they had not previously had to compete, would be successful in pleading that the Dutch be put into the quarters on the islet of Deshima that had been prepared for the Portuguese. Even so, their treatment was considerably better than that accorded Chinese merchants, who had been restricted to Nagasaki earlier, in 1635. The Dutch were worked into the system of attendance at Edo and they dealt with major officials, while the Chinese were without official standing and dealt with low-ranking officials at the port.

Dutch trade at Nagasaki was always smaller in amount than the Chinese trade, and it is in good part the ethnocentricism of the West that has led to our obsession with seclusion when the Nagasaki door was always ajar and sometimes wide open. Ōba Osamu says flatly that "Nagasaki trade was China trade." He argues that historians should see Nagasaki as an international port that functioned as the easternmost point of

---

35. Iwao, "Japanese Foreign Trade," p. 14.

the trade network worked out by Chinese merchants, or as the northernmost point of China's Nanyang trade. To see that trade in isolation, and to concentrate on Nagasaki as only a little window on the wider world, is to perpetuate and accept the sakoku syndrome. Leonard Blussé agrees, pointing to the size and importance of the Chinese trading fleets from Fukien in the years after the Ming lifted the bans on travel overseas by Chinese in the 1560s. Close to a hundred large vessels, containing some 20,000 tons of cargo space, sailed every year to Southeast Asia. "Every year," he writes, "they brought thousands of pieces of silver back from Manila as well as tropical products. At Jacatra [which the Dutch renamed Batavia] the Chinese fleet in the early seventeenth century had a total tonnage as large or larger than that of the whole return fleet of the Dutch East Indian Company." [36]

With the goods came Chinese immigrants, and as the colonies grew a network developed into which the Japanese traders could fit, and, after them, the Europeans. The Chinese chain of trading posts throughout Southeast Asia thus served as the basis for Portuguese, Japanese, and Dutch trading activities in the area. The networks were competitive, but also complementary. Much of the activity that took place can be understood as the securing and maintaining of access routes for the transport of Japanese and New World silver to China and Chinese silks to Japan: more and finer silks for Japanese merchant princes, who supplied the warlord armies of Japan; more richly embroidered garments with family crests for the affluent warriors; and the glories of Momoyama design for the ladies at the daimyo courts who required finer fabric than was available from Nishijin. The rich interiors of Hideyoshi's Fushimi residence, now part of the Nishi Honganji complex in Kyoto, remain as reminders of the opulence that was pos-

36. *Strange Company,* pp. 99, 103, citing Tien Ju-kang and J. C. van Leur.

sible. All of this was served by the China trade. Much of the activity we have parochially thought of as the "expansion of Europe" was European participation in the expansion of East Asia.

To be sure the European contribution was real enough. The introduction of firearms into Japan by the Portuguese created a new thriving industry. Manufacturers in Sakai and other cities produced the weapons that changed the technology and tactics of warfare and speeded the country's unification. It is a remarkable fact that some of these same merchant princes dominated tea taste and often competed with their warrior customers in the acquisition of ceramics and works of art. Firearms led to needs for new imports; for instance, the salt-peter essential to gunpowder was imported from China by way of Siam. Lead for bullets and smelting came by the same route, and so did technical knowledge for building deep-hulled ships capable of long-distance travel.[37] Some imports were of Southeast Asian origin, but the favored product was usually Chinese.

The Commerce

The volume of Chinese trade changed greatly during the Tokugawa period, and even the seventeenth century, when the trade was at its peak, divides into three periods. The opening decades of relative liberality in trade policy were marked by the vigor and then demise of the shuin-sen system. Dutch and English traders were beginning their efforts at Hirado, and the Portuguese were still coming to Nagasaki from Macao.

The Chinese were also coming to Hirado to which, with Nagasaki, the Dutch and English were restricted in 1616. Dutch records provide the best figures for their numbers, for

37. Innes, "The Door Ajar," pp. 82–91.

the VOC tracked its competitors carefully. Dutch and English records show thirty Chinese ships coming to Hirado in 1612, another sixty to seventy in six months of 1614, and seventy to eighty in 1631.[38] The Chinese were helped by a Japanese ban on Dutch ships between 1628 and 1633, a penalty imposed because of the Dutch mistreatment of a Japanese ship on Taiwan. That embargo was rescinded only after the Dutch surrendered Pieter Nuyts, head of the Taiwan station, into Japanese hands in 1632. In 1635 the Chinese were ordered to come only to Nagasaki. Now their numbers grew rapidly; in 1640 seventy-four ships came, and a year later the number grew to ninety-seven.

By this time the trade, though it may have been affected by the poor crop years in China and Japan, was caught up in the political turbulence caused by the Manchu invasion of China. Of the ships that came in 1641, thirteen were under the control of Cheng Chih-lung, a sometime merchant and freebooter whose base of power was in the coastal province of Fukien. Late Ming princes sought support there and proclaimed it their imperial court. Cheng had come to Hirado in 1624 and married a Japanese woman who bore his son Cheng Ch'eng-kung, the famous Koxinga of the Europeans.

The VOC had established itself on Taiwan in 1624, and "Kasteel Zeelandia" became an important entrepot for its trade with Japan and China. The Dutch increased their export of silver from Japan: in 1639, 1,850,000 taels, equivalent to 527,250 florins, were shipped out of Japan by way of Taiwan. Dutch competition with Cheng Chih-lung became intense. He was an important supplier of gold, silk, and piece goods for them, but also a competitor. Nicholas Iquan, as they called him, was so troublesome that one chief factor ended a report to his superiors with the hope that "Iquan, this

38. Ōba Osamu, *Edo jidai no Ni-Chū hiwa* (Tokyo, 1980), p. 30.

thorn in our flesh, be not long for this world!" That wish was soon granted. Iquan shifted to the Manchu side in 1646. He was kept at Peking until it became clear that he could not persuade his son to surrender and, in 1661, was executed. Koxinga proved even more belligerent and drove the Dutch from Taiwan in 1662, depriving the VOC of a major asset.[39]

In the 1640s the Cheng regime actively sought Japanese help against the Manchus. There was strong support for an expedition to China among major Tokugawa collaterals, and inquiries were sent to Korea through Tsushima to ask about the willingness to supply such a force. What stopped the discussion was not so much commitment to seclusion as doubts about the nature of Cheng leadership; the senior Cheng's defection to the Manchu side settled the matter. There was also disenchantment with requests for help from a China that had been standoffish for so long. The Chinese, one daimyo wrote a retainer, "won't allow Japanese ships to approach their shores; they even post picket ships. Therefore it is hardly proper for them to come, now that their country has fallen into civil war, and say, 'We are having some trouble, so would you please send some troops?' " But his next point was even more important: "while it might be proper to respond to them if the request came from the emperor or his general, we don't really know who this messenger is."[40]

Not surprisingly, the disorder on the China coast cut into Sino-Japanese trade. The number of Chinese ships at Nagasaki declined to about fourteen a year during the last decade of the Taiwan resistance. But during the whole of that period most of the Chinese ships that made it to Nagasaki were from territory under the control of the Chengs, from areas controlled by the three feudatories in south China, or from over-

---

39. Yamawaki Teijirō, "The Great Trading Merchants, Cocksinja and His Son," *Acta Asiatica* 30 (1976), p. 108.

40. Quoted in Toby, *State and Diplomacy in Early Modern Japan*, p. 126.

seas Chinese communities in Southeast Asia—that is, from
the resistance. In retaliation, in 1661 the Manchu rulers ordered a withdrawal of the population from coastal areas of
south China in the hope of cutting off supplies from the
Chengs.[41] China was now denied Japanese copper, and Japan
was cut off from easy access to Chinese silk. The Taiwan resistance had been funded in good measure by the export of
sugar and silk to Japan.

The slowdown in trade cannot have been entirely unwelcome to bakufu officials, for Japanese mines were declining in
productivity for lack of adequate technology to control the
rising level of water in pits that became ever deeper. Export of
pure silver ingots was banned at Nagasaki as early as 1609,
although they continued to be sent to Korea for transmission
to China. In 1616 a Nagasaki ginza was established to improve control of silver exports, and subsequent regulations
limited and then stopped the export of objects crafted in silver. In 1668 the bakufu placed a general ban on the export of
silver, and by 1685 it was promoting the export of copper
instead of silver. In 1763 the export of silver was ordered
stopped permanently, and thereafter Japan gradually became
an importer of silver.[42]

In 1683 the Manchus finally managed to gain control of
Taiwan. Now commerce rebounded with a vigor that startled
Japanese officials and drove them to forceful measures of restraint. In 1685 some 85 junks came to Nagasaki; in 1688
there were 193. The result was a dramatic drain of copper out
of the country. Efforts to control the tide of ships led to large-
scale smuggling as ships stood in to other ports or unloaded

41. The best account of this remains John W. Hall, "Notes on the Early Ch'ing
Copper Trade with Japan," *Harvard Journal of Asiatic Studies* 12 (December 1949),
444–461.
42. Tashiro Kazui, "Tsushima han's Korean Trade, 1684–1710," *Acta Asiatica* 30
(1976), 85–105.

offshore. This problem was never solved completely, and there are lively records of Nagasaki investigations of smuggling well into the eighteenth century.[43]

In 1685 the bakufu responded to this unwelcome expansion of trade with the "regulations of the Jōkyō era." Now trade was to be limited to 6,000 kamme (3.75 kg) of copper for the Chinese and half that for the Dutch. Kobata calculates that the bakufu by these measures annually allocated 8,902,000 kin (5,341,200 kg) of copper for overseas trade via Nagasaki.[44] Next came steps against smuggling by establishing control over the Chinese community in Nagasaki. Plans were set in motion for a controlled residence center that would perform the functions that Deshima did for the Dutch, and in 1689 the Chinese residence was established. In its first year it housed 4,888 people when the junk fleet was in. The contrast between this and the minuscule Dutch presence on Deshima is clear. So is the evidence of the quantity of imports. A large fill area was set aside for warehouses to store Chinese goods: it is as conspicuous in pictorial representations of Nagasaki as is the much smaller islet of Deshima.

The Chinese quarter came to occupy an area somewhat larger than seven acres. Its gates locked from the outside. It was surrounded by a palisade and had an inner area surrounded by a moat. On entering the main gate one encountered, on the left, stalls for authorized merchants that provided basic necessities of fruit and vegetables, piece goods, copper utensils, and dishes. On the right were rooms or offices for interpreters, inspectors, headmen, book inspectors, and detainees; these offices were filled in rotation, and occu-

43. Fred G. Notehelfer, "Notes on Kyōhō Smuggling," *Princeton Papers in East Asian Studies*, vol. 1, *Japan* (Princeton, 1972), pp. 1–32.

44. "The Export of Japanese Copper on Chinese and Dutch Ships during the Seventeenth and Early Eighteenth Centuries," summary of paper in Yamamoto, ed., *Proceedings*, pp. 437–438.

pied a small army of over three hundred people. Only prosti-
tutes summoned from the Nagasaki Maruyama quarter were
permitted to cross the moat into the residential quarters,
which consisted of long two-storied barracks (*nagaya*). The
Chinese were allowed to leave the quarter only for authorized
purposes to handle freight, service ships, or visit temples, and
then only when accompanied by Japanese petty officials. So
staffed, the quarter housed an average of two thousand sailors and merchants, the crews of the twenty or thirty junks
that visited Nagasaki annually. In time, however, the severity
of these regulations was moderated, and by late Tokugawa
days it was not unusual to find Chinese traders hawking their
goods on the streets of Nagasaki.

Related to these moves was a succession of changes in the
bakufu administration of foreign trade. Mention has been
made of the itowappu, the early Tokugawa institution that
functioned as a guild of merchants. It was established to present foreign, initially Portuguese, traders with a fixed clientele
of customers who would be able to control purchase prices.
For some time it was circumvented by the shuin-sen and did
not apply to the Dutch, but after removal of the Dutch to
Deshima and the abolition of Japanese trading ships, its powers increased. As disorder on the Chinese mainland rose,
however, so did the price of silk, which was now in short supply, and in 1655 the guild was abolished. There followed a
period of more or less direct trade, but before long prices
were spiraling up under the pressure of competitive bidding.
In 1672 Edo officials ordered that Nagasaki import prices be
posted publicly in Osaka in an effort to lessen speculation.
The regime's desire for a better share of the profits combined
with a search for administrative measures to bring the system
under central control. Provisions for housing all the Chinese
in one place were one expression of this; so were further restrictions on port entry instituted in 1689, under which ship

entry was limited to designated periods of spring and fall. Then, in 1698, came the establishment of the Nagasaki Clearing House (*sō-kanjōsho*), generally called the *kaisho*. Financial accounting for all aspects of foreign trade was now centralized in a single office:—copper barter, innkeeper agents (*funayado*), and allocation of import shares to accredited merchants. For the first time, the bakufu could gain directly from the administration of foreign trade.[45]

The management of China trade under the kaisho is illustrated by Yamawaki Teijirō's summary of the way a junk would have been handled in the late eighteenth century. The sequence was as follows:

—Lookout officer sends runner to bugyō office to announce sighting of ship, its size, description, distance. Other officials alerted. Ship drops anchor outside harbor. Bugyō assigns duties for receiving the ship; some tens of small boats tow it into harbor, where it drops anchor and sounds gong to announce its arrival.

—Party of officials from bugyō office, including inspector of translators, apprentice interpreters, representatives of Chinese residence, and headman of machi responsible for ship [a duty assigned in rotation to Nagasaki streets to equalize profits], board the ship. Formal warnings about Christianity are read, and crew is required to tread on medallion of virgin and child (*fumie*).

—Ship's papers are checked, cargo list and fūsetsugaki presented, crewlist verified. Inventory of aloeswood, ginseng, camphor, and musk submitted. Japanese leave ship.

—Cargo inventory studied in meeting of officials of kaisho, thread guild, machi officials, each receiving a

45. Innes, "The Door Ajar," pp. 278ff.

copy, and contents announced to participating Japanese merchants.

—Following morning, offloading begins, day laborers hired by the machi responsible. Sailors begin to disembark, received by Chinese residence officials at warehouse area. Cargo checked against lists, goods placed in warehouses. Ashigaru guard hovers alongside in small boat. Any items destined for bakufu transferred to Japanese officials immediately.

—Next day, remainder of crew disembarks to enter Chinese residence. Vessel and its firearms, if any, guarded by Japanese.

—Cargo examined in greater detail. Japanese merchants with passes enter compound to examine goods and agree among themselves on reasonable prices. Items so approved are listed and posted. Next morning, bidding begins. Japanese buyers are represented by agents; bids are placed in bags hung beneath the posted commodity. Auctioneer announces three top bids, and Chinese seller negotiates. Seller informs Japanese official of acceptance, and buyer, after examining goods in warehouse, agrees. All sales final.[46]

Chinese purchases from the Japanese were carried out in a similar manner, and the authorization papers for return journeys were given out by the bugyō office immediately prior to the ship's departure. The trade was thus highly institutionalized and carried out with, it would seem, good will and good nature on both sides. The regular rotation of responsibility for ships among the major Nagasaki machi, and the reliance of the city's amusement quarters on patronage from Chinese mariners (who paid lower prices than the Dutch because the entertainers preferred their company), served to underscore

46. *Nagasaki no Tōjin bōeki* (Tokyo, 1964), pp. 297ff.

the fact that foreign trade was the city's lifeline. Moreover, relations between the Chinese and the people of Nagasaki were on the whole friendly. The Chinese were often called *acha-san,* a term of some affection and respect. Major Chinese merchants were seen as generous and wealthy. A giant cauldron was cast for the Sōfukuji (Foochow) temple in 1682 to provide food for victims of the famine of that year, and Chinese curios and songs were popular among the Japanese.[47]

The Restraints

Bakufu measures in restraint of trade began with fears over the outflow of silver, and by the end of the seventeenth century they were extended to copper. The "Shōtoku regulations" instituted by Arai Hakuseki in 1715 tightened the measures introduced in 1685. Now the number of Chinese ships allowed was limited to thirty a year, and permits to enter Nagasaki harbor were limited to ships holding tallies (*shimpai*), which were given to departing junks. The value of permitted exports held steady at the levels set in 1685, though the amount of copper was limited to 3,000,000 kin. Ōba Osamu gives figures [48] for the next century:

1717	40 ships	8,000 kan
1720	30	4,000
1736	25	4,000
1749	15	4,110
1791	10	2,740

Ship numbers alone, of course, can deceive; larger ships could make up some of this difference. But it is clear that exports of

47. Noriko Kamachi, "Chinese in Meiji Japan," in Akira Iriye, ed., *The Chinese and the Japanese: Essays in Political and Cultural Interactions* (Princeton: Princeton University Press, 1980), p. 63.

48. *Edo jidai no Ni-Chū hiwa* (Tokyo, 1980), p. 33.

copper declined sharply. Some of this reduction might have taken place in any case as the result of market forces. At the turn of the century some reports had it that Japanese goods (other than bullion) were so plentiful in central Chinese ports that their prices fell, while the highly prized white silk thread of China was in short supply in Japan because of climatic irregularities in China.

Some coverage of this can be gleaned from the fūsetsugaki that Chinese ship captains, like the Dutch chief factor, were required to file with each arrival. Thanks to this requirement, Japanese authorities had been able to follow the progress of the civil war in China. These reports were forwarded immediately to Edo, as has been noted; they went straight to the top of the authority structure, the council of rōjū. The time lapse was remarkably slight. Reports could make their way from Nagasaki to Edo through the bureaucracy and be in the files there in a matter of about two weeks. This double control on news, Chinese and Dutch, kept the bakufu surprisingly well informed. The Dutch could fudge about happenings in Europe, as they did during the Napoleonic interlude, but when it came to the junk trade, reports from Batavia could be checked against those from China.

Some of these reports submitted by Chinese captains make it clear that officially authorized junks could bypass some regulations so that their official sponsors could enrich themselves (as had been true of bakufu officials and shuin-sen). Taiwan was for a time forbidden to engage in trade even after the Ch'ing court canceled its ban on ocean travel, but officials sent deerskins and sugar to Fukien, where they were included with shipments to Japan. One Foochow captain reported, "Mine is one of a three-junk state convoy out of Foochow. Although the other two carry heavy cargoes of sugar, but no yarns or textiles, mine is a rather large vessel, so I am also carrying yarns and textiles entrusted to me by some officials and merchants in Foochow." [49] Officials were thus, as Toby puts it, piggy-backing on imperially sponsored merchantmen for their own profit. But as soon as prosperity and productivity revived along the China coast, merchantmen from Chekiang and Nanking, where the yarns and textiles originated, seem to have won out again over their competitors from the south in Kwangtung and Fukien.

Clearly "sakoku" had many holes, and they were known to, and at times welcomed by, bakufu and Chinese officials. Seventeenth-century Japan's economy was vitally affected by foreign trade with the rest of East Asia. Nor did it end there; other products from Southeast Asia were transhipped to Korea, and Dutch access to cottons and silks from India and Persia was reflected in consumption patterns in Japan. Despite this, by the eighteenth century most bakufu officials, aware of the dwindling supply of precious metal for coinage, began to see trade as a zero-sum game in which Japan was losing more than could be gained. It seemed urgent to reduce the export of bullion, and that meant reducing Japan's need for imports. A program of what would, in present parlance, be called import substitution was a logical response. Robert Innes provides numerous examples.

In the seventeenth century there had been sporadic efforts to import rare plants, including sugar seedlings and plants suitable for pharmacopoeia, but a sustained and systematic program had to wait for the early eighteenth century. Arai Hakuseki's reports of his discussions with the shogun Ienobu indicate an awareness of the possibility. Ienobu, he writes, said, "If we look back to ancient times, we see that there was no small quantity of goods like medicine produced in Japan.

49. Ōba Osamu and Ronald Toby, " 'Seek Knowledge Throughout the World': International Information and the Formation of Policy in Edo-period Japan and K'ang-hsi Era China," forthcoming in conference volume, "International History of Early-Modern East Asia."

Cotton, tobacco, and the like were not heard of in ancient times, but at present they are produced everywhere. Even so far as commodities never before produced in Japan are concerned, if we obtain the seeds and test the quality of the soil, we can introduce them." [50]

In 1698 Miyazaki Yasusada (Antei), author of the agricultural classic *Nōgyō zensho,* argued the case differently: "Sugar is used in domestic daily life, and so all people, high and low, spend large amounts of money on it. If we find out the right methods to grow cane sugar, then it can certainly be grown successfully in warm provinces on the coast. If we exert ourselves in applying the best technology for sugar cultivation, then we will no longer send Japanese treasure abroad in profligate fashion—which will be a great aid to the country. Whoever exerts himself successfully to promote the cultivation throughout the realm will surely enrich our country forever." But he also pointed out that this would require central direction and support, for "it is beyond the capacity of ordinary people." [51]

The effort would require central direction. It received that from Tokugawa Yoshimune (1684–1751, shogun 1716–1745), who pursued a vigorous policy of economic, especially agricultural, growth. In 1720 he ordered the lord of Kaga to present him with a thousand-odd volume set of botanical lore, the *Shobutsu ruisan,* and the following year he lightened the proscription on books from China, specifying only that they not be about Christianity, in order to make it easier to learn from Chinese botany.

This had consequences for more than plants. When Yoshimune first ordered his *shomotsu bugyō* to bring him all the

50. *Told Round a Brushwood Fire: The Autobiography of Arai Hakuseki,* trans. Joyce Ackroyd (Princeton: Princeton University Press, 1979), p. 180.

51. Quoted in Ōba and Toby, " 'Seek Knowledge Throughout the World,' " p. 40.

Chinese gazetteers in the Momijiyama library, they numbered only twelve. In the next fifteen years 412 titles were added. The gazetteers were studied for ways in which to increase Japan's agricultural productivity. With this came a program to investigate Japan's botanical resources for parallels with Chinese flora, to order seeds and seedlings, and to experiment with local plantings. We find Yoshimune ordering Matsuoka Gentatsu, a Kyoto savant, to come to the Kanto area to identify pharmacological plants. He also invited a Soochow physician, Ch'en Chen-chien, to Nagasaki in 1722 to investigate the countryside around Nagasaki and identify plants; five years later two more Chinese doctors were hired to compile a list of botanical equivalents for Chinese plants. Then came experimental stations; one at Koishikawa was five acres in size. Orders were sent to Nagasaki to question Chinese on the cultivation of ginseng and sugar cane, and Satsuma was instructed to divulge its knowledge of sugar refining. Soon seedlings from Ryūkyū were growing in the grounds of the Hama Detached Palace, in Musashi, and in Suruga as well as in Nagasaki. Yoshimune also distributed seedlings to daimyo throughout the country with instructions to try the plants out in their areas. In the early nineteenth century Ogawa Yasushi looked back on this and remembered when "all the sugar was imported from foreign lands. But now it is produced in Kii and in Shikoku; they are even making crystal sugar. It is not the least inferior to imported sugar . . . confectioners have been using it exclusively."[52]

Yoshimune was able to use the commerce with China to satisfy personal whim as well as larger goals. In 1728 Ship Number Nineteen brought a pair of elephants from Annam. The captain lacked a tally authorizing his entry, but he was on safe ground because he knew of an order that Yoshimune

---

52. Ibid., and Ōba, *Ni-Chū hiwa*, pp. 224ff, where the author uses the Meiji term for "foreign employees" (*Kyōhō no oyatoi gaijin*).

had sent out several years earlier, by way of a ship bound for Siam, for a pair of albino elephants. Each elephant had a Vietnamese handler. The Nagasaki report describing the animals went into exuberant detail. Unfortunately the female died a few months after arrival, but before long plans were underway to move the surviving male to Edo.

The greatest of care was taken with the beast's presumed sensibilities. All along the route directions were issued to make sure that the elephant would not be disturbed or panicked. People were to be allowed to gather to see him at intersections, but not along the roads. It was permissible to follow the procession, but not to get in front of it. No one was to look down on the animal from a second-story window or balcony. Quiet was to be maintained.

The entourage, accompanied by the Nagasaki bugyō and followed by local headmen, left Nagasaki in the third month and reached Kyoto at the end of that month. In Kyoto arrangements were made so that a curious sovereign, Nakamikado Tennō, and the retired emperor Reigen could see this marvelous apparition. This entailed a problem, however, since no one without court rank could be received in audience. The solution was to grant the elephant Fourth Imperial Rank (a status that put him higher than most daimyo) with the designation "Annam White Elephant, Fourth Rank" (*Ju-yon'i Kōnan Hakuzō*). Now ennobled, the beast could perform the obeisances in which his handlers had coached him. He was rewarded with sake, a hundred-odd bean-jam buns, and a hundred tangerines. Court nobles vied to greet the event with poems, and the procession lumbered on to Edo.

In Edo the elephant was put up in the Hama Detached Palace grounds before being led to Chiyoda Castle with proper pomp for a visit with Yoshimune. In the few months of life that remained to him—he died in 1730—the elephant was the talk of the town, the subject of admiration for writers and their publishers, and a source of income for enterprising vendors, who concocted cure-all potions from his waste. All this bespeaks a relaxed and peaceful atmosphere.[53]

Yoshimune's measures for limiting imports were accompanied by sumptuary legislation designed to discourage ostentation and waste. But these, repeated in each successive period of reform, are probably best read backward, as seen in a mirror, reflecting things that were actually going on. Nor did the measures to increase productivity necessarily help the bakufu. More often than not, they strengthened the local economy of the domain in which they succeeded, changing its strength relative to that of its neighbors. Satsuma, for one, gained far more from sugar production than did the central government, since this product, on which it enjoyed a climatic monopoly, gave it a secure source of income that helped to finance the political and military structure so important in the Meiji Restoration.

Innes argues that a similar pattern resulted from the greatest import-substitution program of them all, the encouragement of sericulture. Bakufu and daimyo policy converged to create an industry that freed Japan from its dependence on Chinese silk. The growth of the Nishijin weaving sector in Kyoto provides a startling example. The quarter consisted of a guild of only 31 households in the early sixteenth century. By Genroku times it had grown to become a community that, including dependents and workers, numbered more than 70,000 people. As late as 1715 Nishijin was still working with thread imported from China, but domestic prosperity and improved craftsmanship, both fueled by the ever-expanding Japanese market, allowed Japanese silk to take over.

53. Ōba, *Ni-Chū hiwa*, pp. 160–183. When the Dutch, in sterner times, tried to curry favor by sending an elephant as tribute in 1813, the Senior Council brusquely rejected it as something of no use (*muyō*) and ordered them to take it back.

Before long, the primacy of the Nishijin weavers was un-
challenged. Neither sumptuary regulations nor cost pre-
vented the steady spread of silk through Japanese society.
"Ever since some ingenious Kyoto creatures started the fashion," Saikaku wrote, "every variety of splendid material has
been used for men's and women's clothes, and the draper's
sample books have blossomed in a riot of color"[54] At higher
levels of society, this was going on even before Saikaku wrote
about his luxury-loving townsmen. The shogun Hidetada's
daughter Kazuko (Tōfuku mon'in), the wife of Go Mizunoo
Tennō and mother of the Empress Meishō, seems to have had
lavish tastes in fashion: she ordered 340 items costing a total
of 150 kan of silver from the draper Kariganeya in the six
months before her death. Edo's decision to establish traditional court ceremony ensured that Kyoto (and its weavers'
guild) would have a leading place in Japanese fashion. By
Genroku times, seven Kyoto clothiers served the shogunal
household as official purveyors, and over 160 more served
daimyo from all parts of Japan.

Imported yarn may have been the favored product up to
the Genroku years, but a bakufu order in 1713 for weavers to
use domestic yarn probably signals the turn. As domestic sericulture became widespread in Hokuriku, Tōsan, and Kantō,
the weaving industry began to be dispersed. Nishijin began to
lose its edge for all but the most elaborate and expensive
products. So widespread was the diffusion of sericulture that,
by the nineteenth century, bakufu attempts to channel or re-
strict domestic trade in silk by ordering it funneled through
the great shogunal city guilds were being successfully sub-
verted by regional entrepreneurs and their political sponsors.
When the ports opened to foreign trade in 1859, Japan's silk

54. *The Japanese Family Storehouse or The Millionaire's Gospel Modernised*,
translated from the "Nippon Eitai-gura" of Ihara Saikaku by G. W. Sargent (Cambridge: Cambridge University Press, 1959), p. 26.

exports quickly became a powerful source of profit, strengthening the economy in general but weakening the bakufu's ability to monopolize profits from the exchange.

THE CHINA TRADE, then, was an important factor in the political and economic history of both China and Japan in the seventeenth century. It financed much of the resistance of Taiwan and south China to the Manchu takeover. It provided luxury goods for a growing Japanese market whose elite wanted more of everything the ships could bring. It helped to consume the impressive stocks of precious metal that Japanese had mined during the consolidation of political power.

As those stocks diminished, Japanese authorities became concerned by the flow of metal outward. Just as they were becoming aware of this, the lifting of restrictions on trade that followed the Manchu victory produced such a flood of ships and commodities that the bakufu had to clamp down. The regulations of 1685 and 1715 reduced the flow of commerce at Nagasaki and foretold a decline in the Korea trade. The only possible long-range solution was the encouragement of domestic production of such import items as silk, sugar, and ginseng. Yoshimune, credited by historians with lifting the restrictions on books, was in reality trying to institute restrictions on imports. In some respects these events have a curiously contemporary flavor and relevance.

Section of map of Nagasaki, 1802 woodblock. The legend indicates distance to other cities, symbols for offices of town elders, and daimyo guard stations. The Chinese residence is at the corner of the larger legend block; warehouses for the China trade are separated by bridges to the south and east. Left of center, the fan-shaped island fill is Deshima, magnified in scale. A Dutch ship, towed by two lines of small boats, fires a salute on entering the harbor; the ship behind it is identified as coming from Fukien.

肥前崎陽　玉浦風景之図

Three sections of a sixfold woodprint of Nagasaki by the Yokohama artist Sadahide, 1862. The folds shown here depict warehouses for the China trade and Deshima, with the Maruyama pleasure quarters at the right.

Chinese prints influenced Japanese printmakers in their depicition of Nagasaki. This one, of Soochow, is in the Namban Bijutsukan, Kobe.

Votive painting (*ema*) of a Suminokura shuin ship, dated 1634, donated to the Kiyo-mizu Temple, Kyoto, in supplication for safe travel and prosperity.

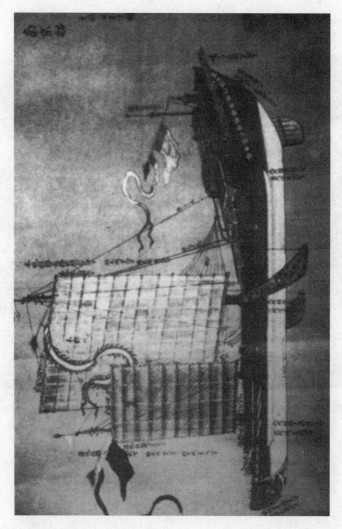

A Nanking ship. In actuality this is a Hangchow Bay trader: a flat-bottomed, high-pooped river ship with cotton sails and leeboard bulwarks on each side of the mainmast.

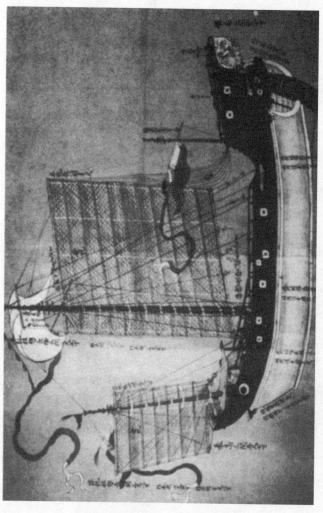

A Ningpo ship. Ships from Ningpo, Foochow, Taiwan, and Canton, though different in size, were all painted black above the waterline; their keels were a brilliant white with a caulk line to prevent leaking. Below the cotton topsail was a sail of matting arranged diagonally on a network of bamboo and rope.

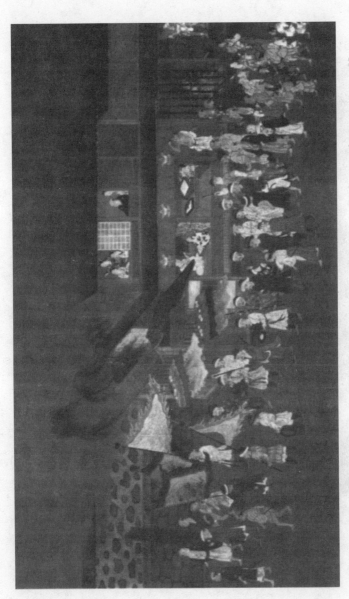

Scroll by the bakufu painter Kanō Harumizu, presented by the shogun to the house of Mito in 1740. Upon arrival in Nagasaki, processions carried the ship's image of the goddess Matsu to the Chinese temples, where ceremonies of thanks for the safe voyage were held. Here we see lines of celebrants from two ships; representatives of the bugyō are in the lead, followed by interpreters and town elders in solemn tread, all watched and accompanied by other Japanese.

The Kōfukuji, or Nanking, Temple in Nagasaki. Until 1734, all the chief priests were Chinese.

Scroll depicting the late eighteenth-century China trade at Nagasaki. In the Matsuura Historical Museum, Hirado, ascribed to Hirowatari Koshū, a painter trained in the Shen Nan-p'in school.

A particularly fine example of Ming architecture: Kaisano ("Opening the Mountain" or Con-secration Hall), Mampukuji Temple, near Uji.

2 Dimensions of the Image

"NAGASAKI," the eighteenth-century Confucian scholar Ogyū observed, "is a place where eastern barbarians [Japanese] and Chinese associate, where ocean-sailing ships come to port; it is the port of a myriad goods and strange objects, where people from the five directions gather, abandoning their homes and coveting profit; it is the first place of our land." [1] It was a city full of temptation and false values, but it did provide access to real, living Chinese. Having discussed the nature of the physical contact between Chinese and Japanese at Nagasaki, it now becomes possible to talk about some dimensions of the image of China in the Tokugawa period. How did the actual contacts affect that image?

This is not an easy question. There is no reason to be sure that what we can identify as Chinese in origin seemed that to all Japanese. It is reasonable to think that varied greatly by social class, especially with the opportunity for literacy and sophistication. Sinologists like Ogyū, who devoted their lives to teaching and writing about ancient, which to them meant Chinese, civilization and who tried desperately to associate themselves with that heritage, were in a different category from less-lettered samurai whose values may have centered

1. Quoted in Olof G. Lidin, *The Life of Ogyū Sorai, a Tokugawa Confucian Philosopher* (Lund: Scandinavian Institute of Asian Studies, 1973), p. 120.

on fighting spirit, and both were even more removed from unlettered farmers whose horizons were restricted to the valley in which they lived. That is why I speak of "dimensions": there was no single image. Still less was there a single China.

Let us begin with the awareness that a small fraction of the thousands of Chinese who came to Nagasaki were important out of all proportion to their numbers, and that a small fraction of the cargoes on the junks counted for more than most of the silks and deerskins. I mean by that the priests and teachers, along with the books they brought. That should probably be pleasing to us as students and teachers as we remember how insignificant a proportion of the total contact with other countries we ourselves constitute, though it is probably also true that the pervasive nature of the cultural contact of our own day—especially in the realm of popular culture—provides few guidelines for comparison with early modern China and Japan. As we shall see with Ogyū and other intellectuals, in an age of relative isolation the very possibility of cultural contact could arouse intense enthusiasm and excitement.

Yet one can scarcely get beyond mere impressions of contact and influence. It is extraordinarily difficult to locate evidence of specific influence, and harder still to evaluate it. There are any number of studies of Chinese influence in literature and art, but it is not easy to decide what this meant for the images held by most Japanese. But one can begin with what went into some of the views and attitudes, and look for examples among image makers, in some cases, and image consumers in others.

People

The junks from China brought people as well as books, and not all of them were merchants and sailors. Chinese junks in the Southeast Asian trade, as Leonard Blussé points out, had cabins on deck, and they were frequently crowded with passengers. Few of the sketches that Japanese made of junks in the Nagasaki trade show the passenger space of those bound for Southeast Asia, but they did bring people, and some of those people were interesting and important.

Mention has been made of the specialists who came on invitation from the shogun Yoshimune in the first quarter of the eighteenth century. Ōba Osamu, as I mentioned, uses for them the term used for foreign employees in the Meiji period, *oyatoi gaikokujin*, hired foreigners. Yoshimune's interests ranged from the calendar to botany to medicine, and though he focused principally on the import-substitution program, that was not the end of it. Ōba provides the names and records of a number of scholars, doctors, and veterinarians.

Some important men came on their own or at the invitation of the Chinese living in Nagasaki. There was a remarkable number of Zen monks. The Zen Master Yin-yüan ("Ingen", 1592–1673) came to Nagasaki in 1654 at the invitation of the "Nanking" temple. He was already the superior of the Wan-fu-szu (Mampukuji) temple on Mt. Huang-p'o (Ōbaku) in Fukien, having been invited to Japan earlier by Japanese monks who deplored the state to which the Rinzai sect seemed to have fallen. The abbot brought a number of disciples with him, teachings calling for a more literal interpretation of the Buddhist precepts, and a revised ordination ceremony. Soon he had gained the attention of the abbot of the Kyoto Myōshinji, Ryōkei (1602–1670), and shortly after that he was invited to Kyoto where he had audiences with the retired emperor Go Mizunoo, the longest-lived sovereign before Hirohito; he also gained the patronage of the shogun Tokugawa Ietsuna. With this backing he was able to obtain permission for the construction of the Mampukuji in present-day Ōbaku, outside Uji (see illustration).

Construction began in 1661 and was completed in 1669. The name was taken from Ingen's Fukien temple, and the site was chosen because of the abundance of Ōbaku trees, a genus credited with medicinal properties and also producing a yellow dye for paper and textiles. In embellishment and plan the inspiration is entirely Chinese, and the Mampukuji complex provides the best surviving example of Ming Buddhist architecture. Its design and decoration were done in good measure by craftsmen who came from China. Mampukuji came to serve as the main center for Rinzai Zen, and a 1974 Agency of Cultural Affairs survey credited it with 478 branch temples, 458 priests, and 244,584 adherents.

The China connection continued long after the temple's dedication. All Mampukuji abbots were Chinese from the parent temple in Fukien until 1740, and after that Chinese abbots alternated with Japanese clerics until the end of the eighteenth century. Mampukuji ritual retained southern Chinese influence, and even the recitation of sutras is said to retain traces of Fukienese pronunciation.

Mampukuji monks were welcome at the highest levels of Edo society. Their coming coincided with the religious and cultural enthusiasms of the court of Tokugawa Tsunayoshi (fifth shogun, 1680–1709) with its legislation ordering compassion for all living things (*shōrui awaremi no rei*) and its efforts to cultivate manners by moralistic injunction.[2] Tsunayoshi's subordinate Yanagisawa Yoshiyasu has had a bad press from Confucian historians but, in addition to appointing Ogyū Sorai as one of his house scholars, he was particularly active in attracting Chinese monks. He welcomed to his residence a number of Chinese Ōbaku monks, as well as Jap-

2. Donald H. Shively, "Tokugawa Tsunayoshi, the Genroku Shogun," in Albert M. Craig and Donald H. Shively, eds., *Personality in Japanese History* (Berkeley: University of California Press, 1970), and Beatrice Bodart Bailey, "The Laws of Compassion," *Monumenta Nipponica* 40:2 (Tokyo, 1985), 163–189.

anese from Nagasaki who were scholars of colloquial Chinese, and even started his own study of colloquial Chinese. One product of this was a series of meetings, some of them attended by the shogun himself, at which talks on Confucian classics were given in Chinese. This was the setting in which Ogyū developed his own study of modern Chinese. No doubt the discussion was stilted and artificial, but the interest in China was real enough and reminds us of the enthusiasm for Chinese dress and objects at the court of the Muromachi shoguns three centuries earlier.

The abbot Yüeh-shan, whom the Japanese know as Eppō, came to Nagasaki in 1657 and to Edo in 1705. There he was hosted in the shogun's Chiyoda Castle for a question-and-answer session at which Japanese Zen priests interpreted; the story has it that Yanagisawa was the only one present who found it unnecessary to wait for the interpreters. It was to Eppō that Ogyū wrote in 1707, to express his gratification in having met his "compassionate and gracious person. We had a marvelous conversation on various subjects. It was like the playing of bells; when they sounded high, inquiries were answered; when they sounded low, there were gasping sounds. The brushes flew over the paper creating a wind, the ink came down on paper producing flowers . . . Now, untiringly and diligently, you presented me with your beautiful teaching . . . Returning home, I felt close to fainting and was filled with memories . . . I have just tasted the sweetest taste of sweets, it still sticks to my teeth and cheeks, and I cannot get it rinsed from my mouth." [3] The flattery is heavy, but the respect is real. Clearly the Chinese was wonderful to hear ("the playing of bells") hard to produce ("gasping sounds"), and inadequate for communication ("brushes flew over the paper").

In some of this correspondence one begins to see support

3. Lidin, *Life of Ogyū Sorai*, p. 117.

for, if not indeed the origins of, Sorai's strong belief in the necessity of getting away from Sung scholarship and back to the ancient texts. Another Ōbaku priest, Kōgaku, received equally fulsome praise for a session in which "I listened to your expostulation, and together we discussed and examined the upper and lower one thousand years [of Chinese history] . . . The language and literature because of this becomes easy to understand . . . The age, carrying the language with it, changes; the sounds having their limits, depend on the soil." And to yet another Ōbaku priest Sorai wrote, "Now, at a time when Confucianism was on the decline, I unfortunately became a Confucianist. However, at a time that the Way of Buddha had come across the Sōrei mountains, you, Roshi, fortunately became a Confucianist." Thus these personal contacts played an significant role in the development of the thought of the man sometimes considered Tokugawa Japan's foremost philosopher.

Nagasaki scholars of Chinese also made their way to Edo to take part in these discussions and found respect and companionship in the circle of Genroku scholars. Sorai sent disciples to study with them and used them as guides for his own spoken Chinese. He wrote a friend that "their clothes and caps were Japanese, but their words and smiles were Chinese. There was nothing about them that was not amazing. In our land of sixty-six provinces, by means of what combined spirit were people like them created? . . . When we investigate [pronunciation] thoroughly, we necessarily make old and modern times come clear."[4] Sorai made a sharp distinction between these scholars and what he knew of the regular Nagasaki interpreters, who seemed to him bureaucratic poseurs. "To cough in a clear and detailed fashion like the Chinese, and to chirp and to grit one's teeth like the Chinese, how can that be

4. Ibid., p. 120.

called the Art of the Way?" In the nineteenth century we find
the Edo circle of specialists in Dutch studies equally unenthu-
siastic about the Nagasaki interpreters, no doubt partly because the latter guarded their knowledge as a scarce commodity on which they had a monopoly. What counts, though, is
the contrast between the kind of professional advice and
practical coaching that was accessible to the Edo circle of Sin-
ophiles and the much greater difficulty that scholars of Dutch
learning had in making first-hand contact with European men
of learning. For the latter, language learning and translation
had to be carried out on a trial-and-error basis, and it is no
accident that one of the first monuments of the later age of
translation took the form of explanatory notes on a volume
of anatomical tables for which only the illustrations had provided clues to meaning.

In the same years that Ōbaku Buddhism was reaching Japan, a number of loyalist Ming Confucianists were seeking
assistance and refuge. It will be remembered that a request for
military assistance against the Manchu invasion received se-
rious consideration from the Edo government in the 1640s,
only to be rejected after it became clear that the southern
cause was foundering. In 1642 a staunch Ming loyalist arrived at Nagasaki in the person of Chu Shun-shui, who fled
China in 1642 and moved for some years between Nagasaki,
Annam, and Siam—the trading routes of Chinese junks—
seeking help against the Manchus. In 1644 he abandoned
these hopes and applied for refuge. At Nagasaki he was met
by a retainer of Tokugawa Mitsukuni who offered him em-
ployment in Mito. From then until 1682, when he died in
Edo, he helped with Mitsukuni's projected history of Japan,
the *Dai Nihonshi*. This work, organized in the manner of the
Chinese dynastic histories, further followed their example by
focusing on the imperial court, and while it stopped short of
taking the story on into Tokugawa times, its emphasis and its

influence on shorter and more popular versions played a role in the revival of loyalist sentiment. It was also an appropriate undertaking for the peaceful years of Genroku, for Tsuna-yoshi styled himself something of a Confucian sage-king as well as a compassionate Buddhist. He sponsored efforts to identify and restore the tombs of former emperors, as a result of which attribution was standardized for 66 of the 78 "imperial" tombs, and sponsored a renewal of the Great Harvest Festival (*Daijōsai*) rites that had not been performed since the fifteenth century.[5]

The influence of Chinese expatriates and visitors was as important in art as it was in religion and thought. In the years between the establishment of the Chinese quarter in Nagasaki and the end of Tokugawa rule, some 130 Chinese painters came to Nagasaki. Few of them were professionals; most were priests or merchants whose skill came to the attention of the Japanese. Like the merchants, most of them were from the centers of of bourgeois culture in the Yangtze basin and from provincial centers along the southeastern coast. They were the products of a nonaristocratic culture that had been developing since Sung times and that came to some sort of flower in Ming days. They were well prepared to enrich the taste of well-to-do and cultured Japanese townsmen. The principal figures are Ch'en Yuan-yun, who arrived in 1638 and stayed fifty-two years; I, Fu-chiu, who came in 1720, journeyed regularly between Japan and China, and is last recorded in 1747; Shen Nan-p'in, who came in 1731 and again in 1733; and Sung Tzu-yen, a disciple of Shen Nan-p'in, who taught at Nagasaki from 1758 to 1760. Of these only Shen Nan-p'in had a career that can be traced clearly. He was a professional painter with a good reputation that, tradition has it, led to an invitation from the king of Ryūkyū, but he went to Japan instead. Upon his return he played a significant role in the

5. Kate Wildman Nakai, *Shogunal Politics: Arai Hakuseki and the Premises of Tokugawa Rule* (Cambridge: Harvard University Press, 1988), p. 182.

art world of central China and sent many of his paintings to Japan, where they were highly regarded and eagerly sought.[6]

Such painters made two contributions to Japanese art of the early modern period. They introduced the Ming and Ch'ing school of bird and flower painting, a genre of gentle scenes of nature that soon became popular in Japan. Shen Nan-p'in sent back much of his work to Japan, where some five hundred items, of which two hundred are considered reliable attributions, survived. They also introduced literati (*bunjinga*) painting to Japan and had a discernible influence on the work of artists like Yosa Buson and Ike no Taiga. In the eclecticism of late Tokugawa art, painters as different as Watanabe Kazan, Tani Bunchō, and Tanomura Chikuden all drew on these paintings. Sinophilism reached an apogee in the work of some painters who, like Ki Baitei (1734–1810), were so devoted to their Chinese teachers and models that they took Chinese names for themselves. It is possible to say, as Stephen Addis does, that they brought a "new vision" to Japanese art.[7]

As literati art developed, it flowed into a fluid and eclectic-style that contributed to many parts of Edo life. Tani Bunchō began in the Kanō school, studied under a devotee of Shen Nan-pi'n, and later, because of his skill in rendering landscapes, was commissioned by Matsudaira Sadanobu to paint natural sites appropriate for gun emplacements. In these he also incorporated elements of perspective. This "western"

6. Biography in *Chūgoku no kaiga: raihaku gajin,* ed. Kobara Kōshin (Tokyo, 1986), p. 6; catalogue of an exhibit at the Shibuya Shōtō Museum. I owe this reference to Yoshiaki Shimizu.

7. Stephen Addis, ed., *Japanese Quest for a New Vision: The Impact of Visiting Chinese Painters, 1600–1900* (University of Kansas: Spencer Museum of Art, 1986). Ralph Crozier has pointed out that some of this vision returned to China a century later in the works of Canton School painters who sought new ideas in Japan. *Art and Revolution in Modern China: The Lingnan (Cantonese) School of Painting, 1906–1951* (Berkeley: University of California Press, 1988).

approach also came by way of Nagasaki, but apparently through Chinese prototypes, well in advance of the late eighteenth-century Japanese study of European art from books brought by the Dutch.[8]

Tanomura Chikuden (1770–1835), who came from a family of physicians, studied Ming treatises on painting and became a close friend of Rai San'yō after his lord made him official domain historian. He later resigned that post in protest against the lord's suppression of a peasant rebellion. Still later he became the favorite painter of Kido Takayoshi, whose diary entries are replete with expressions of esteem for this versatile painter's style. Perhaps the best example of all of the flow of cultural influences is seen in Shiba Kōkan (1738–1818), who studied the Chinese bird and flower techniques in Nagasaki and took a Chinese name; he then shifted to genre art and took a new name, evocative of Harunobu, his new model, before turning to Western styles. These in turn led him to undertake a trip to Nagasaki. Haga Tōru's recent reissue of Kōkan's Nagasaki travel diary makes it inviting to study this representative of late Edo eclecticism. Throughout, however, Kōkan prided himself on his mastery of "thin ink washes in the Chinese manner."[9] Clearly Kōkan's Japan was not very "closed."

There are a number of reflections about cultural inter-

8. See the documentation provided by Henry D. Smith II in "World Without Walls: Kuwagata Keisai's Panoramic Vision of Japan," in Gail Lee Bernstein and Haruhiro Fukui, eds., *Japan and the World: Essays in Japanese History and Politics in Honour of Ishida Takeshi* (Oxford: Oxford University Press, 1988), p. 254, n. 7. Smith states: "(Maruyama) Ōkyo became the first in Japan regularly to apply Western techniques of landscape perspective, a method he apparently learned from Chinese adaptation of European originals" (p. 8). His source is Julian Jinn Lee, "The Origin and Development of Japanese Landscape Prints: A Study in the Synthesis of Eastern and Western Art," dissertation (University of Washington, 1977), chaps. 4 and 5.

9. Calvin L. French, *Shiba Kōkan: Artist, Innovator, and Pioneer in the Westernization of Japan* (New York and Tokyo, 1974), and Haga Tōru and Ōta Rieko, eds., *Kōkan saiyū nikki* (Tokyo, 1986).

change that can be made in connection with these painters from China. The first is that, with the exception of Shen
Nan-p'in, they do not figure in the mainstream of Chinese
artists. One looks in vain for their names in the annals of
"eminent Chinese" that we have for Ming and Ch'ing times.
In an insular Japan, however, they were nevertheless warmly
greeted by people of considerable importance. Ike no Taiga
developed an ardent admiration for one of I Fu-chiu's painting, and Hosoi Heishū, a prominent Confucian teacher whose
sermons make him an interesting example for the diffusion of
more-or-less Confucian teaching, esteemed him as well. But
conventional art history has little good to say about this
work. Ernest Fenollosa, whose esteem for Kanō formalism
blinded him to everything else, dismissed even the literati
painting of Taiga and Buson as "hardly more than an awk-
ward joke," and Alexander Soper writes of Shen Nan-p'in as
"a Chinese of no great ability . . . whose painting of birds and
flowers were pretty in colour and truthful in intent." [10]

These Chinese teachers were indeed unlike the elite scholar-
aesthetes in China. I Fu-chiu was in fact a merchant, and he
came to Japan first as a shipping broker. The journey was
occasioned by nothing more ethereal than delivery of a cargo
of horses ordered by the shogun Yoshimune, held up because
of a Ch'ing ban on horse exports during a military emergency
related to a campaign in the northwest. The young broker—I
Fu-chiu was then only twenty-three—managed to evade officials by sailing at night. Mishaps brought his ship to shore in
Satsuma, but with help he made it to Nagasaki and entered
port on the strength of a permit issued to his brother. In the
years that followed he continued to go back and forth to Nagasaki; he last appears in Japanese records in 1747. Creden-

10. Ernest Fenollosa, *Epochs of Chinese and Japanese Art* (New York: Dover,
1963), vol. 2, p. 165, and Robert Treat Paine and Alexander Soper, *The Art and
Architecture of Japan* (London: Macmillan, 1955), p. 122.

tials of his sort, however, whatever they tell about his courage and business acumen, do not qualify him for inclusion among the usual company of artists we read about.

Nevertheless Nagasaki painters, largely unknown in China, became famous in Japan. Their importance lies in what they helped to stimulate, not in what they produced within their own tradition. It is their association with later masters, such as Tani Bunchō and Tanomura Chikuden, that counts; I Fu-chiu, for instance, is honored as one of the "four great masters from abroad." He and the others were to have many nineteenth-century successors, the Western teachers who assume heroic stature in Japanese memory but get short shrift in Western biographical dictionaries. L. L. Janes, William Elliot Griffis, and even Fenollosa are of interest to us primarily because of their influence on their more important students. For those of us who are teachers that is probably not a discouraging thought.

Along with the bird and flower schools of Ming-Ch'ing painting there was Chinese music for entertainment, known as "Ming-Ch'ing music," which became popular first in Nagasaki and gained somewhat wider currency in Tokugawa and Meiji times. The lyrics were sung in the Chinese original, with pronunciation indicated in Japanese phonetics in the margins. Rulan Chao Pian writes: "The abundance of printed scores and texts of such songs, which today can still be found in old book shops in Japan from time to time, point to their popularity once in Japan. As late as the 1960s there were still elderly performers in Nagasaki who remembered these songs, and the pieces that they performed were perfectly recognizable to any Chinese who knows the songs at all."[11]

11. "Interrelationships of the Musics of East Asia: Japan, Korea, China, Vietnam and Mongolia," 1988 manuscript. See also Noriko Kamachi: "A Chinese song, 'K'an-k'an hsi' (Look!), sung by courtesans in the central dialect, was about a ring made of nine small rings. Such songs, with a Japanese verse attached, were very pop-

Law and precedent

The Tokugawa shoguns Ieyasu, Tsunayoshi, and Yoshimune, who wanted to structure and stabilize their society, had an intense interest in finding appropriate models for social and institutional engineering. When these seemed to exist in periods of stability in the past, they were usually Chinese in origin. When more recent foreign examples seemed appropriate, they were still Chinese. In either case the administrative codes of China provided the most appropriate models for emulation. But finding, understanding, and implementing them required careful preparation. In this context government sponsorship for scholarship, sometimes binational in character, provided another avenue for the influence of Chinese civilization.

Almost two decades ago Dan Fenno Henderson pointed out that Tokugawa studies of Ming law marked a third period, with Nara and Meiji, of Japanese law; they led to a recovery of much of the administrative record that was lost in the disorder of Japan's feudal centuries. Ōba's more recent work continues and enriches the survey begun by Henderson, who had only the first of the Ōba works at hand.[12]

Ieyasu began his search for literature on law and precedent very early, for it was relevant to his regulation of the court nobility. Precedent could resolve disputes about procedure. But it proved difficult to find people competent in Nara and Heian *ritsu-ryō* precedents, to say nothing of Chinese law. The first gains were made in the late seventeenth century in

ular among the Japanese in Nagasaki." From "Chinese in Meiji Japan," in Akira Iriye, ed., *The Chinese and the Japanese* (Princeton: Princeton University Press, 1980), p. 63.

12. Henderson, "Chinese Legal Studies in Early 18th Century Japan: Scholars and Sources," *Journal of Asian Studies* 30 (November 1970), 21–56, and Ōba, *Edo jidai ni okeru Chūgoku bunka juyō no kenkyū* (Tokyo, 1984), pp. 233–263.

Tsunayoshi's time, and they were helped by the presence in Japan of Ming emigré scholars and the progeny of Koreans who had been part of the forced population movement during Hideyoshi's invasions. Maeda Tsunanori (d. 1724), daimyo of Kaga, and Hosokawa Shigekata of Kumamoto (d. 1785) provided important support from their own domains. Concerned with the practical problems of rule, they were drawn to the apparent comprehensiveness of Chinese examples, particularly in penal codes. Yoshimune, as daimyo of Wakayama in 1705–1716, benefited from this interest as well, for Wakayama scholars had done some of the first commentaries on Ming law. At Edo the shogun Tokugawa Ienobu encouraged his minister Arai Hakuseki in parallel efforts to acquire the Ming codes of law through Nagasaki. Maeda Tsunanori sent two of his retainers to Edo to consult Chu Shun-shui while he was working there for Tokugawa Mitsukuni, and he also searched vigorously for Japan's early codes. In a letter written in 1711 he complained, "Alas, Japan's codes are gone! I simply do not find any." The same letter, addressed to a Kyoto aristocrat, asked politely whether "you happen to have the eight works listed on an accompanying sheet. If not I earnestly hope that you will ask the cooperation of someone who does happen to have them." One is reminded here of the efforts of "Dutch" scholars, and their daimyo, to secure copies of rare Western works a century later.

It is fascinating, and perhaps for us encouraging, to see how difficult these texts were for eighteenth-century Japanese, despite their formidable grasp of Chinese. The same Maeda Tsunanori, after a talk with Muro Kyūsō, noted that "there were things in the Code that were impossible to understand. Accordingly questions were put to Koreans, as a result of which some degree of understanding was gained. There can be no comprehension by sole reliance on textual commentary without oral transmission." Maeda went on to quote a phrase and then said, "Since no one had any idea what it meant, the question was put to Koreans, among others, and at length some understanding was gained." [13]

A half century later scholars, without much help from oral transmission, had a comparable struggle with Dutch. Unlike the students of Chinese law, however, the work on Western texts began privately, and much of it continued without official subsidy. The work on Chinese administrative codes was carried out with official sponsorship and even supervision. The *Tokugawa jikki* for 1721 notes:

> This day, in the presence of Toda Yamashiro-no-kami Tadazane [a rōjū], Matsudaira Kai-no-kami Yoshisato summoned the jushin Ogyū Sōemon Shigekuni and commanded him to translate the *Liu yü yen-i* [amplification of the six maxims]. This book was [transmitted by] a Ryūkyū islander, Tei Junsoku (Ch'eng Shun-tse), presented on an earlier occasion by Matsudaira Satsuma-no-kami [Shimazu] Yoshitaka. [14]

What is involved here is the Six Maxims first issued by the Ming founding emperor T'ai-tsu in 1398, expanded and commented on toward the end of the dynasty by a village teacher named Fan Hung, who added appropriate stories, poems, and legal cases to drive home the points. The result was published and frequently reprinted in late Ming and early Ch'ing times, as a desirable homily for inculcating public virtue. Six simple precepts enjoined respect for parents, for elders and superiors, harmony in the village, instruction for children and grandchildren, contentment with one's lot and livelihood, and abstention from wrong. This little set of maxims, enriched by Fan Hung's commentary, came to Satsuma from Okinawa in

13. Henderson, "Chinese Legal Studies," p. 33
14. Ibid., p. 37

vernacular Chinese, was thence forwarded to the shogun, and was considered a suitable assignment for Ogyū Sorai.

Moral pronouncements of this sort played an important role in the normative posture of Confucian rulers. The Six Maxims were reissued by the first Manchu ruler, Shun-chih, in 1652, and expanded to sixteen in the Sacred Edict of K'ang-hsi in 1670. His successor, the Yung-chêng emperor, in turn issued his own exposition of the Sacred Edict in 1724. Throughout the Ch'ing period these injunctions served as basic texts for the system of rural lectures (*Hsiang-yüeh*) that made what Hsiao Kung-chuan termed "Imperial Confucianism" central to rural order.[15]

Surely there is a relationship between this transmission and the use of Confucian moralism to strengthen the respect for authority in Edo Japan. Yoshimune ordered a simplified translation of the *Liu yü yen-i* prepared for use in lower schools. There are records of lords who ordered village leaders to explain its virtues on the first day of every month, and the work was reprinted many times into the Meiji period. The Six Maxims, moreover, made "no mention of loyalty to the emperor, and in that sense they may have commended themselves to Tokugawa rulers."[16] Most daimyo were happy to attract traveling lecturers like Hosoi Heishū to lecture on morals and submission to authority.[17] Hosoi's key point was

15. *Rural China: Imperial Control in the Nineteenth Century* (Seattle: University of Washington Press, 1960), pp. 184–191.

16. Tao De-min, "Traditional Chinese Social Ethics in Japan, 1721–1943," *Gest Library Journal* 4:2 (Princeton, 1991). Tao notes also that in 1943 the Sinologue Ogaeri Yoshio published a new edition of the commentaries of the Six Maxims and Sacred Edict with a preface explaining that it was "one of the editor's favorite books; he offers it to those who want to play an active part in Greater East Asia"—in other words, it could still be useful for governing Manchuria and China.

17. R. P. Dore, *Education in Tokugawa Japan* (Berkeley: University of California Press, 1965), pp. 238–241, and Michiko Y. Aoki and Margaret B. Dardess, "The Popularization of Samurai Values: A Sermon by Hosoi Heishū", *Monumenta Nipponica* 21.4, (Winter 1976), 393–413.

contentment with one's lot and appreciation for the concern shown by those who ruled. That these talks, despite their banality, provided welcome breaks in a monotonous routine of village existence is suggested by Hosoi's account of his triumphant tour of Yonezawa. After a talk in a village called Komatsu, Dore quotes his assurance that the villagers "were all choked with tears, and especially the older men were so sad to see me go that when I left for Yonezawa 700 or 800 of them prostrated themselves in the snow and wept aloud." No doubt one should make allowance for a countryside so quiet that, as one popular saying had it, on summer evenings people sat outside listening to the ants.

There is a clear link between these injunctions and the larger diffusion of Confucian morality in Edo times and the reverential position that was accorded the 1890 Imperial Rescript on Education in imperial Japan. Prior to its formulation, the Ministry of Education had tried to make use of Tokugawa texts on Confucian morals that built on the *Liu yü yen-i,* but without much success. In the debate that preceded the rescript in 1890, the conservative scholar Nishimura Shigeki held up the K'ang-hsi and Yung-cheng imperial precedents as arguments for compiling morals textbooks directly within the imperial household, and in the end the rescript was issued without the countersignature of a cabinet minister in order to create the impression that it was the work of the Meiji emperor himself.[18] The rescript made room for the requirements of a contemporary participatory society, but it centered on the exhortation that "Ye, Our subjects, be filial to your parents, affectionate to your brothers and sisters; as husbands and wives be harmonious, as friends true; bear

18. For the early attempts, see Kaigo Tokiomi, *Kyōiku chokugo seiritsushi no kenkyū* (Tokyo, 1960) p. 74; for Nishimura, Donald H. Shively, "Motoda Eifu: Confucian Lecturer to the Meiji Emperor," in David S. Nivison and Arthur F. Wright, eds., *Confucianism in Action* (Stanford: Stanford University Press, 1959), p. 329.

yourselves in modesty and moderation; extend your benevolence to all." Having the principal read this in school was a
reasonable substitute for the earlier gatherings of respectfully
attentive villagers.

Yoshimune's encouragement of the study of Ming law led
to the publication of Sorai's commentary on the Ming code in
1725, to further studies in T'ang law, and to major projects
devoted to the *Ta Ch'ing hui tien*. Here again we should note
the difficulty of the texts for Edo Japanese who did not know
their context. Ogyū Sorai was not one to minimize his
achievement:

> The book of the Ch'ing code is equally difficult for all
> local scholars. This is because scholars of our country do
> not understand the Chinese usage. Furthermore, even the
> Nagasaki interpreters cannot cope with the code because
> there are many technical terms of the government offices.
> I myself struggled mightily with the Ming code. Then I
> read from various sources and was able to master the
> system of the bureaucracy . . . until I knew it as clearly as
> the palm of my hand.[19]

Of a T'ang source that Yoshimune received from the Konoe
family in Kyoto, the *Jikki* notes that it was sent back to China
by way of a merchant who presented it to the prefect of the
Ch'ing Board of Punishments, who declared it very rare and
had a copy made for himself.

Direct access to Chinese nationals at Nagasaki was important to the scholarly achievements of most of the official projects at Edo. Ch'en Hsieh-an, who came to Nagasaki in 1727,
was, in Ōba's view, probably the finest scholar of the group.
It was he who worked with the Japanese on the recension of
the T'ang work later sent to China. From 1727 to 1731 he

19. Henderson, "Chinese Legal Studies," p. 38.

was allowed to live outside the Nagasaki Chinese residence, the sort of concession made for von Siebold in the 1820s but not to other visiting foreigners. Upon Ch'en's departure for China in 1731, he was given special privileges in the form of shipping permits and a gift of silver from the shogun. In 1736 he returned to Nagasaki for a second visit, accompanied by his grandson. Thus much of the work I have described can be characterized as a binational effort. It is not difficult to imagine the number of Japanese sinologues that Ch'en interacted with in Nagasaki; his poems appear in a number of local anthologies. Another interesting case is provided by the scholar Fukami Kyūdayu, the grandson of a Chinese immigrant, who served Yoshimune by spending time in Nagasaki getting books, editing a version of the *Ta Ch'ing hui tien,* and who was finally appointed commissioner of books (*goshomotsu bugyō*).

Books

The import of books was a major part of the Nagasaki trade. Books constituted a small proportion of the goods imported when the trade was at its height, but as the Japanese need for goods diminished and literacy grew, the Japanese appetite for books increased. The interest in Chinese institutions shown in studies of law and precedence could not have been satisfied without access to Chinese books and the ability to order additional titles through Nagasaki. The scholarship of Ōba Osamu has opened up an entire field of study for the history of cultural contact.[20]

20. Ōba's *Edo jidai ni okeru Tōsen mochiwatarisho no kenkyū* (Kyoto, 1967) is richly documented and remains the basic study, supplemented and in places updated by his more inclusive *Edo jidai ni okeru Chūgoku bunka juyō no kenkyū* and the anecdotal, but no less rigorous, *Edo jidai no Ni-Chū hiwa.* In addition there are a number of monographic and documentary publications issued by his Kansai University.

Records are complete only for the year 1711. Of the fifty-four ships that came from China that year, five carried books, which made up less than 10 percent of the cargo. In the troubled years of the south Chinese and Taiwanese resistance to the Manchu invasion, books became fewer because the centers of publishing in China were no longer as accessible. But thereafter, although trade declined and fewer ships came to Nagasaki, more and more of them were likely to carry books. In 1804 two of the eleven Chinese ships that arrived carried books; by the mid-nineteenth century, virtually all of them did. In Ch'ing times Kiangsi and Chekiang were leading centers of publishing, and as "Nanking" ships came to predominate, Nagasaki had access to the best.

The bakufu was from the first aware of the importance of Chinese books, both positively and negatively. Educated Japanese could be expected to be literate in Chinese, and bakufu encouragement of Confucian studies gave relevance to such imports. But the restrictions on religion and thought that accompanied the seclusion measures of the 1630s raised problems as well, for it was important to stop Christianity at the water's edge. In China the Jesuits and their followers had transmitted current European science, particularly astronomy, and their writings were banned whether or not they dealt with Christianity.

Censorship of Chinese began with an assignment to a temple established in Nagasaki by the bakufu. Soon two book dealers were coopted as well, and in 1639 Mukai Genshō, a Saga Confucianist who had served as physician and also taught, was appointed to bakufu office. His successors maintained that position through at least seven generations. Book dealers were required to execute a pledge that began with gratitude to the authorities and a pledge to support the polity (*kōgi*) and observe the ordinances, and went on to promise to report the appearance at Nagasaki of any works concerning military matters, Christianity, or "anything unusual" (*mezurashiki shomotsu*), whether at Edo, Kyōto, Ōsaka, Sakai, or any other place. A list of banned works was circulated to book dealers and is found in the miscellaneous papers of a number of Tokugawa intellectuals, indicating their predictable curiosity about the forbidden.

Ōba gives a number of illustrations to show how the system worked. One is impressed by its formality and thoroughness: an alarm is raised, the investigation leads to interrogation of the ship's officers and crew who offended by including the work in their cargo, the officials have a formal hearing, and the verdict specifies the penalty. Thus in 1685 Mukai Gensei spotted the Chinese translation of a work by a Jesuit that attacked Confucianism, Taoism, and Buddhism. The paper trail of the process is remarkable for the exactitude of the inquiry; the result was the burning of the offending book, seizure of the rest of the cargo, and exclusion of the shipowner from further trade at Nagasaki. Mukai's reward was promotion and formal appointment, with a succession right to the office for his descendants.

Naturally he continued vigilant. In 1695 a guidebook to Peking arrived, entitled *Ti-ching ching-wu lüeh* (J. Teikyō keimono ryaku), which made mention of the site of the former Catholic cathedral and, worse, Matteo Ricci's tomb. Again the hearings, briefs, and documentation are impressive. So was the outcome: permanent loss of the right to travel to Japan for the shipowner and captain. Of course some resorted to subterfuge. Ōba, even more alert than Mukai, discovered in the collection of the Fukuyama domain a curious work, the "Seven Overcomings," a translation of a Jesuit morality book on overcoming seven vices, which had apparently been smuggled in by altering—or rather dismantling—the Chinese characters of its title to read, nonsensically, "Sixty-one and ten elder brothers." Had it been discovered earlier, this could have been a dangerous game.[21]

The Nagasaki censorship system could also serve a positive function. It gave bakufu officials the first chance at incoming materials and made it easy for authorities to know what was available for their own order lists. The growth of major daimyo collections and of the bakufu's Momijiyama library would have been much more difficult and haphazard without some locally based post of observation. In the nineteenth century, as pressure from the outside world began to mount, the system worked to give bakufu officials quick access to important books. The Nagasaki bureaucrats tended to be cautious and protective, and to be on the safe side they usually covered themselves by sending Edo cryptic summaries of books they were not quite sure about. This in turn made it possible for their superiors at the capital to spot items that were of special relevance. By the 1840s, these censorship provisions were useful in alerting high officials to military problems.

Wei Yüan (1794–1856) was the author of two works of great importance in alerting nineteenth-century Japanese to the danger of the West. His *Hai-kuo t'u-chih,* a geographical discussion of maritime countries, was based upon work begun by Commissioner Lin Tse-hsü, the official disgraced by China's defeat at the hands of the English. It was published in fifty fascicles in 1844, again in sixty fascicles in 1849, and expanded to a hundred in 1852. When three sets of the 1844 edition reached Nagasaki in 1851, the censor Mukai Geki thought it might be dangerous and requested instructions from his superiors. They ordered him to send the sets along, but by the time he received these instructions he had to report

---

21. Such skills did not die. One is reminded of the medical bookstore outside the gate of the Imperial University in prewar Tokyo that shelved Lenin's *Left-Wing Communism: An Infantile Disorder* under Pediatrics.

that they were already in the hands of the Edo authorities. One was in the possession of the rōjū Makino Tadamasa. Soon two other rōjū had copies, and when another fifteen sets arrived in 1854 seven were brought by bakufu leaders and eight went on sale to the public. Soon the book's discussion of "America" was published in Japan, clearly to exploit interest roused by Perry's arrival, and before long other sections began to appear under the editorship of Shionoya Tōin, a sinologue who drew on it to express his fear and loathing of the West,[22] and Mitsukuri Rinshō, a student of Dutch learning. Thus a work that the Nagasaki bureaucrat would have preferred to ban quickly gained national attention within five years of its arrival at Nagasaki.

This was even more the case with another work by Wei Yüan, "Imperial Military Exploits" (*Sheng-wu-chi*), which discussed the Ch'ing experience in border conflicts and rebellions. The book received immediate attention, and with remarkable speed. It was written in 1842, reached Nagasaki in 1844, and was snapped up by the head of the Senior Council, rōjū Abe Masahiro. A second copy was soon in the hands of another rōjū, Makino Tadamasa. Within the year two more copies were imported for the other two members of the council. In 1848 eight more came, this time to be put on sale. Within two years, three Japanese editions had been published. In short order these works were in the hands of leading Edo officials as well as samurai intellectuals, who learned from them a lively fear of Western expansion. Yoshida Shōin, Sakuma Zōzan, and other late Tokugawa activists wrote of their anxiety and indignation after becoming familiar with these books. As alarm grew, the speed of transmission accelerated. A collection of poems lamenting the destruction of a naval base by English forces, *Cha-pu chi-yung*, published in

22. See R. H. van Gulik, "Kakkaron: A Japanese Echo of the Opium War," *Monumenta Serica* 4 (1939), 478–545.

1846, was brought to Japan that same year, in twenty-four copies.[23]

The import of Chinese books to Nagasaki, then, was a vitally important part of the trade, and it had a profound impact on Japanese intellectual and political history. It added immeasurably to Japan's holdings in all forms of publications from China, from provincial gazetteers to botany and technology. In 1721, after Yoshimune's relaxation of the prohibition on books affected by the West, it became possible to import works on science, astronomy, and geography—many, admittedly, already dated in the Europe where they were produced. As the nineteenth century brought new concerns about Western expansion, the introduction of current Chinese discussions of war and defense brought home to samurai intellectuals the imminence of threats to the country and helped to draw them into politics.

China as Civilization, Country, and Metaphor

One would expect the image of China to be particularly complex among Tokugawa intellectuals. Literacy and education for the elite were thought of in terms of the mastery of Chinese, and a disproportionate amount of time was spent teaching students to read texts in classical Chinese. In the main this was done by rearranging the lines to conform with the principles of Japanese syntax, adding markers to indicate the sequence in which characters were to be read and indicating grammatical signifiers as required. This was a cumbersome process that, in effect, converted Chinese to Japanese when successful. Even when it was not, with luck it might give some idea of the meaning.[24] At higher levels of scholarship and so-

---

23. Ōba discusses these books and their influence in *Ni-Chū hiwa*, pp. 242–247.

24. Modest education could produce modest results. Of Sakamoto Ryōma, a nineteenth-century activist, we read that he proudly showed a friend his mastery by

ciety, on the other hand, full literacy in Chinese was a must. Ogyū Sorai insisted on the necessity of reading Chinese as written. Shoguns and daimyo maintained Confucian scholars at their administrative centers who taught and lectured on problems of statecraft from the Chinese classics. Study, moral cultivation, and reflection were taken very seriously, certainly by the scholars and frequently by their rulers, and assumed an importance that was religious in nature.

Some years ago Kate Wildman Nakai discussed some of the problematic relationships these scholars had with the China that was so central to their specialization.[25] Most "professional" Confucianists, she points out, were people "whose status in Tokugawa society was fraught with ambiguity, who looked to Confucianism not for a means of justifying and upholding their position as it was, but for a means of changing it, or at least resolving some of its ambiguities." Usually of modest rank, often sons of doctors or of rōnin, they were marginal to the elite they taught. The China whose texts they expounded was ideally a single-class society in which the scholar-official provided the ideal type, but the society in which they lived was one of rigid class lines topped by a hereditary military caste in which they could participate only at the pleasure of their superiors. The scholar Arai Hakuseki (1657–1725), Kate Nakai points out, recalled that in his youth people in a position of power tended to look down on Confucian scholars with suspicion, almost as if they were Christians. Thus the Confucianists faced the problem of na-

---

reading aloud, at the top of his lungs, a copy of the *Tzu-chih t'ung-chien,* paying no attention to the punctuation indicated. " 'Do you mean to say you can understand it that way?' asked the startled visitor. 'Well,' said Sakamoto, 'I get the general idea.' " Marius B. Jansen, *Sakamoto Ryōma and the Meiji Restoration* (Princeton: Princeton University Press, 1961), p. 88.

25. "The Nationalization of Confucianism in Tokugawa Japan: The Problem of Sinocentrism," *Harvard Journal of Asiatic Studies* 40 (June 1980), 157–199.

tionalizing and universalizing the values of their texts without appearing to deracinate themselves.

Their first task was to show that the way of the sages was universal, not exclusively Chinese, and that it had meaning for Japan as well. Since, after all, the Confucianists were more conscious of the Chinese origin of their teachings than most of their contemporaries, they needed to separate Confucianism from China. The Way, Kumazawa Banzan argued, was not restricted to one country, and Asami Keisai assured his readers, "Whether seen from the perspective of the Chinese, ourselves, or the Indians, no one will claim that it is his Way alone. If, reading Confucian works one says, 'It is the Way of China! The Way of China!' and mistakenly feels that one should surrender to them, customs and all, without reserve, one does so out of failure to perceive the true principles of heaven and earth and out of narrowness of observation." Arai Hakuseki agreed: "Where is the place that a sage cannot be born? How could it be that it was only in the so-called 'flowery kingdom' that sages were born?" Even Ogyū Sorai, who styled himself an "Eastern barbarian" (thereby incurring harsh criticism from later loyalists), wrote that "the reason why China is the country of the rites and their practice is because of this ability to think"; he tended, Nakai says, "to universalize the sages by detaching them from the China of later ages" and by asserting that his personal understanding of their teachings was superior.

Clearly these efforts were only partly successful, and the almost poignant efforts of these men to win the approval of Chinese scholars—Hakuseki for his poetry, as he tried to have samples sent to China, or Sorai in his struggle with contemporary colloquial Chinese and his obsequiousness to Ōbaku priests—indicated their insecurity. Robert Borgen's description of the way tenth-century Japanese court officials tried to compete with Korean ambassadors in writing Chinese poetry shows that this insecurity was by no means new.[26]

A subsequent stage was one of competition with the Chinese originals, by emphasizing areas in which Japan might be considered superior to China. Yamaga Sokō cited the imperial lineage as evidence for the higher degree of benevolence and righteousness of Japanese rulers, adding that Japanese military exploits in Korea established Japan's superiority. There followed the logical argument that true Confucian institutions had been preserved in Japan but abandoned in the unitary empire of China. In China, Sorai's student Dazai Shundai argued, the bond between rulers and people had been broken, while Japanese feudalism had preserved them. Tokugawa institutions were, in fact, "precisely the system of the three [Chinese] dynasties. How wonderful!"

It could then be maintained that China had degenerated while Japan remained pure. China had been invaded and conquered by the barbarian Manchus of the north, and it no longer made sense to refer to China as the "central efflorescence." Ogyū Sorai found it inappropriate to refer to the legal code as that of the "Great" Ming dynasty, since it had fallen, and suggested instead that it was entirely proper for Japanese to claim the signifier Great (*Dai*) themselves. Yamaga Sokō went on to conclude that *chū* (central) probably fitted Japan more precisely than it did China; the Way of the Sages was better upheld in Japan than in China, and geographically Japan, surrounded by the four seas, was stronger than a China surrounded and periodically conquered by the four barbarians. As one goes on to nineteenth-century nationalists among the Mito Confucian scholars, one finds Aizawa Seishisai (1781–1863) quietly appropriating for Japan the term "Cen-

26. *Sugawara no Michizane and the Early Heian Court* (Cambridge: Harvard University Press, 1986), pp. 139–40.

tral Country," making a "crucially important shift in world view from universal empire (*tenka*) to nation-state (*kokka*), a perceptual shift that would take decades longer in China."[27]

For the true elite of Tokugawa Japan, the rulers and aristocrats, it is probably correct to say that "China" remained an ideal land of sages and tranquillity. The Kanō school of art favored by the shogunate and most of the daimyo adorned its screens and scrolls with representations of an idyllic world peopled by figures who, as the stock phrase had it, never felt winter's cold or hunger's pangs. Even today it is striking to see how faithfully the surviving panel paintings of Hideyoshi's Fushimi Castle in Kyoto, and the paintings of the Kanō masters in the great Kyoto temples, transmit this image of a land that never was. For the patrons of these artists China, as the point of origin for so many Japanese cultural standards, had to be reverently depicted in a utopian setting. The Tokyo Kōrakuen, laid out for the Mito daimyo Tokugawa Yorifusa and Mitsukuni, has a path winding along the shore of the Western Lake of Hangchow, a lake created by excavating soil and reassembling it in the shape of a Lushan the daimyo had never seen. Comparable evocations of distant grandeur were echoed in many smaller daimyo estates.

The tide of poetry in Chinese, a tradition that dated back to earlier centuries, swelled in the Tokugawa period and may have exceeded what was being written that in Japanese. Authors of *kanshi,* Chinese poems, found the genre a good vehicle for expression of ideas poorly served by the shorter, evocative verse forms of Japanese poetry. Kanshi do not seem to have flourished during the first century of Tokugawa rule; the mastery of Chinese was not yet widespread, and the early sinologues sternly derogated the writing of poetry as a form

27. Bob Tadashi Wakabayashi, *Anti-Foreignism and Western Learning in Early-Modern Japan: The New Theses of 1825* (Cambridge: Harvard University Press, 1986), p. 9.

of dilettantism. In the eighteenth century, however, Ogyū Sorai and other Confucianists preened themselves on their ability to write poetry in Chinese. Thereafter a widespread enthusiasm for kanshi as vehicles for realistic, sometimes even satirical, expression grew. By the early nineteenth century, Chinese poetry was serving to convey nationalist and political dialogue, and many of the leading figures of late Tokugawa politics prided themselves on their Chinese verse. This enthusiasm continued into the Meiji period. Irokawa Daikichi shows how even rural, nonsamurai village leaders expressed their emotions and concerns in Chinese poems. Some sent their compositions to urban masters, who charged by the line for corrections, and government leaders joined with poets in kanshi groupings that crossed the usual lines of social and political division.[28]

For those with genuine yearning to further such cultural leanings, the opportunity came in the Meiji period after the establishment of the Ch'ing mission in Tokyo in 1877. Sanetō Keishū's discovery of the papers of Ōkōchi Teruna, the former Matsudaira daimyo of Terasaki, revealed how strong this desire was. The published record shows that perhaps one-fifth of the "conversations" carried out by brush between Ōkōchi and Chinese Minister Ho Ju-chang consisted of expressions of the daimyo's enthusiasm for the supposedly superior culture of his friend's country. Ōkōchi apologizes for his small islands, far less splendid than the great land the en-

28. See Burton Watson, *Japanese Literature in Chinese*, vol. 2, *Poetry and Prose in Chinese by Japanese Writers of the Later Period* (New York: Columbia University Press, 1976); Donald Keene, "The Survival of Chinese Literary Tradition in the Meiji Era," in Yue-him Tam, ed., *Sino-Japanese Cultural Interchange: Aspects of Literature and Language Learning,* Papers of the International Symposium on Sino-Japanese Cultural Interchange, vol. 2 (Chinese University of Hong Kong, 1985), pp. 75–90; and Irokawa Daikichi, *The Culture of the Meiji Period*, ed. Marius B. Jansen (Princeton: Princeton University Press, 1985), pp. 123ff, "Poetry in Chinese and Revolutionary Thought."

voy has left behind. He is tireless with suggestions for ways
that the Chinese might take advantage of plums, cherries, and
autumn leaves for occasions that could be celebrated in Chinese verse. Ōkōchi is also scornful of his government's course
of modernization (he was, after all, a Tokugawa retainer) and
rebuffs the efforts of the Chinese minister to learn more about
it by saying that he has no knowledge of and less interest in
the group now in power. What he seeks is Chinese culture,
and that in a setting of aristocratic leisure. It is startling to see
the strength of nostalgia in this man, recently a feudal lord,
and his professed indifference to politics, especially when only
a decade before he had been a military commissioner, *rikugun
bugyō*, in the bakufu's abortive efforts to modernize itself.
Clearly sinophile emotions ran strong.[29]

That being so, the first target of the polemic that nativist
scholars directed against their Confucian contemporaries had
to be China. Establishment scholars like Yamaga Sokō and
Aizawa Seishisai might claim for Japan the centrality that had
always been asserted for China, but the scholars of national
learning (*kokugakusha*) of the eighteenth and nineteenth centuries carried this farther by rejecting much of Chinese culture
as well. It was not enough for Motoori Norinaga and Hirata
Atsutane to deprecate the Manchus or to assert that the Japanese, as the inheritors of Chinese civilization, had carried it
to new heights. In his *Naobi no mitama* of 1771 Motoori
inveighed against the entire cultural tradition associated with
the Sages. China was a country of disorder and violence, he
argued, and the so-called Sages were nothing more than successful practitioners of a special brand of deceit. It might be
useful to study Chinese books, but only after grounding in
Japanese values enabled one to recognize the full error of the
Way of China.

29. Sanetō Keishū, *Ōkōchi bunsho: Meiji Ni-Chū bunkajin no kōyū* (Tokyo,
1964).

The nativists were using, and not describing, China. Harry Harootunian's argument that China served as metaphor, that the "use of China in discourse had nothing to do with the way Japanese perceived China, but it had everything to do with the way by which writers related the world of things in specific modalities," is to the point here.[30] Motoori and the others were far from ignorant of the Chinese tradition they criticized, and Motoori in particular was himself influenced by techniques of philological analysis that his sinological contemporaries had developed. No doubt he was also profoundly irritated by Japanese Confucianists with their pedantic worship of the imported tradition. Essentially, China served as the Other: it represented form and structure in contrast to the natural and the spontaneous; normative morality in contrast to the intuitive and the free; ponderous prose in contrast to the lyrical and evocative poetry of Japan. Motoori's China was a dehistoricized and nonexisting country, as indeed it was for the Confucianists who lamented their cultural distance from it. Once the kokugaku scholars had dethroned the powerful pull of Chinese civilization, their disciples could go on to denigrate it further or claim, with Hirata Atsutane, that Japan's spirit and learning were in fact superior since they had incorporated whatever was of value in the Chinese original. In a sense the very excesses of one outlook, in which China served as apotheosis of the good, led to the other, which found in that same China an exemplar of error.

Among Tokugawa commoners, however, China remained or perhaps became a country. As the years of peace brought with them urbanization, literacy, and a popular culture expressive of quotidian concerns and gratifications, one senses a decided gap between the official, scholarly, and elite mode of expression and the more popular view. I am sure there was

30. "The Functions of China in Tokugawa Thought," in Iriye, ed., *The Chinese and the Japanese*, pp. 9–36.

movement between the two worlds in both directions; the popular view of the Other finds an echo in the vitriolic polemics of the kokugaku scholars, just as the growing self-satisfaction of the samurai moralists, and their moral code, was transmitted to ordinary people through the stage and kana books. Irokawa Daikichi has it that popular views of China were overwhelmingly favorable and respectful until the late Meiji period, and that it was the movement of thousands of Japanese farmboys to the continent in the wars of 1894 and 1904 that brought about change. The letters, diaries, and tales of disease and distress that these young men brought home, he feels, helped to account for the twentieth-century Japanese scorn of "Shina" as a backward and dirty land. Surely that large-scale contact, quite without precedent, did help to solidify and diffuse such attitudes. But there were also preparations for them in Tokugawa times.

To take a single cultural artifact as an example, Chikamatsu's puppet play of 1715, *Kokusenya gassen* (translated as *The Battles of Coxinga*), can serve us well. This favorite of the Japanese stage is as frank a statement of Japanese military and moral superiority over China as one can imagine. The hero Cheng Ch'eng-kung is part Japanese, and Chikamatsu dubs him Watōnai, "between China and Japan," to indicate this mixed parentage. He is more than a match for his opponents, who are a cowardly rabble. The audience is reminded of the expedition sent to Korea by the legendary Empress Jingū; Japan's military prowess has been long established. The Chinese do not fight particularly well, although they are decent people. What is deplorable is that they are about to be conquered by the barbarian Manchus. "This land," a Ming general laments, "this land which has given birth to the sages will soon fall under the yoke of Mongolia, and we shall become their slaves, differing from animals only in that we do not wag tails or have bodies covered with fur." Watōnai's pent-up fury gives way in a withering blast that is also self-revealing. He shouts: "Vile creatures! You who despise the Japanese for coming from a small country—have you learned now the meaning of Japanese prowess, before which even tigers tremble?" His sword, "imbued with the strength of the Japanese gods," is so powerful that it would not be fair to use it. Still he cannot resist using a sacred charm from the Great Shrine at Ise. As victory follows, the narrator intones, "How awesome is the majestic power of the Goddess Amaterasu!" It is presumably beside the point that this is supposed to take place outside Nanking, where Koxinga was in fact defeated in 1659 with heavy losses, and irrelevant that he died shortly afterward in 1662, although not before seizing the Dutch fortress on Taiwan. But it is worth noting that he was posthumously reclaimed for China and restored to honor by the Ch'ing court in 1875, probably as a result of the Japanese invasion of Taiwan the year before.[31]

No doubt it would be a mistake to make too much of this. But it would be even more of a mistake to ignore it as simply small-country chauvinism. The crowds that thronged the theaters to see this drama year after year clearly relished the contrast between Japanese courage and Chinese pusillanimity—they were well aware that China was a regional superpower and Japan was not, and they liked seeing their side win.

Finally, it can be contended that in the popular view China gradually became less a specific geographic location and instead served as a metaphor for the "other" or "outside." Ronald Toby has been studying popular perceptions of outsiders in the Tokugawa period. One of his themes is that the term

31. I use the splendid translation by Donald Keene, *The Battles of Coxinga,* in his *Major Plays of Chikamatsu* (New York: Columbia University Press, 1961). Keene also discusses the play's nuances of meaning in "Confucianism in Tokugawa Literature," in Peter Nosco, ed., *Confucianism and Tokugawa Culture* (Princeton: Princeton University Press, 1984), pp. 131–134.

Tōjin, which we encountered in the Nagasaki terminology for traders and interpreters, came to represent an undifferentiated, all-purpose "other."[32] In early Tokugawa times there was still a variety of terms for outsiders; Xavier was thought to be an Indian (*Tenjikujin*, reversing, as Toby puts it, Columbus' error); Europeans were first lumped as *nanbanjin* (southern barbarians) and then differentiated as allowance was made for northern Europeans as *Kōmōjin* (red hairs). With the Ming collapse and the Manchu conquest of China, however, Chinese were lumped as natives of T'ang (Tōjin), and then by the end of the century Kaempfer, on his trip to Edo, reported commoners shouting "Tōjin! Tōjin!" as he passed along the road. By late Tokugawa times foreigners of all stripes, including Americans and English, were lumped as Tōjin. In Shimoda, it may be remembered, the young woman who served Townsend Harris was ostracized by her contemporaries as Tōjin Okichi.

Ōba suggests that the term *Tōjin* was by no means complimentary, in that it dismissed the millennium of Chinese history that followed the T'ang as irrelevant and denied the existence of the contemporary Chinese dynasty by never referring to it as "Shinkoku." This may be overstated, for others point out that in Fukien dialect the term was standard. Whatever the case, *Tōjin* clearly became a general term for foreigner, postulating a "this" Japan against any "other."

There is a larger point here, which is that in the Tokugawa period the Japanese first became fully aware of themselves as a national entity. In Ryūkyū and Hokkaido a few edges remained fuzzy, to be sure, but by and large the full incorporation of marginal provinces and minorities into a stratified whole was a process completed in early modern times. The elite had long been self-consciously Japanese; the experience

32. "Kinsei Nihon no shōmin bunka ni awareru Chōsen tsūshinshizō: sezoku, shūkyōjō no hyōgen," *Kan* 110 (July 1988), 106–158.

of emissaries to China in T'ang times and the warrior response to the Mongol threat in the Kamakura period shows that, but it was in the Tokugawa years that everybody else came aboard. In this sense the slow incorporation of even the Ōbaku establishment through the alternation of Japanese and Chinese abbots, and finally the elimination of the Chinese, carried the same message. As that happened, given the setting in which the appearance of outsiders became more structured and less frequent, their otherness became more conspicuous and, for the untutored, ludicrous. "Don't laugh," regulations warned on the occasion of Ryūkyūan or Korean embassies. Even at the highest levels of society, as Kaempfer discovered when he was ordered to amuse his hosts at the shogun's court in various demeaning ways, the code might better read, "Let's laugh."

Tōjin was not the only term of disrespect that outsiders were to encounter. It is worth noting that Saigō Takamori, during his island exile in the 1860s, referred to the Ryūkyāns around him as *ketōjin*, literally "dirty Chinese" (though the *Kenkyūsha* 1974 edition defines it as "white man, a Westerner"). Then there is the appearance of the term *chankoro*, which was being applied to the Chinese community in Nagasaki by the early nineteenth century. Here the etymologies offered are entirely insulting, with a range from female sex organs to the clink of small coins. In Meiji times the addition of *bōzu*, for the shaved tonsure around the queue, did little to improve things. One could go on to a range of related idioms, such as *Tōjinkotoba* for "nonsensical sound." The vast majority of idioms related to *Tō* or *Kara* also turn on the unprofitable or the meaningless.

It is true that, in the process of nation building in early modern and modern times, the differentiation of self from other has been inevitable in all countries. Because in Japan it came at the same time that kokugaku nativism was postulat-

ing an undifferentiated "this" for Japan as linguistically and
ethnically pure and special, and because Japan was more se-
cluded, it may have been more virulent. Perhaps this mind-set
helps to account for the alacrity with which nineteenth-
century Japan was prepared to "part with Asia," in Fukuzawa's words, and join the circle of imperialist powers.

Late Tokugawa

In the late eighteenth century, a new awareness of China as a
country entered Japanese consciousness. For a brief period it
related to considerations of national defense against China,
and thereafter it concentrated on China's failures in military
matters. Since military considerations had been set aside after
the consolidation of Ch'ing power on the mainland and were
irrelevant during the peaceful decades of the eighteenth century, it comes as something of a surprise to see how quickly
the seventeenth-century misgivings about Manchu power
were revived among Japanese writers who thought about national defense. Some reminders of China as a country were
the products of defensive positions adopted by intellectuals
concerned with Western studies. Sugita Gempaku (1733–
1817), for instance, responded to criticisms that he was
studying the learning of remote countries that knew nothing
of the sages by arguing that China itself was only one country
in the Eastern Sea, and under barbarian rule at that. But others posited a threat from China.

Hayashi Shihei (1738–1793) began his *Kaikoku heidan* in
1786 and completed it in 1791. His alarm for his country had
been stirred by the sudden appearance of the Hungarian ad-
venturer Baron Moritz A. von Benyowsky in 1771 with his
warnings of a Russian attack, but his concern for aggression
from Russia was tempered by his knowledge of the distance

involved. His real fear was China, which, he noted, "is not the China of yesterday." Strong rulers like K'ang-hsi, Yung-cheng, and Ch'ien-lung had pacified the country and doubled its size by force of arms. For the first time China's inner Asian boundaries were secure, and consequently the Manchus were free to face east. Japan was once again, as it had been in Mongol times, in danger from barbarians who would have little respect for its superior virtue and morality. It needed to prepare for this possibility with a rapid development of its own maritime capability in ships and cannon along European lines.[33]

Forty years later, the Chinese danger seemed part of a larger pattern of aggression that was discerned by Watanabe Kazan (1793–1841), who developed a much more thoughtful and comprehensive framework for thinking about China. Like the scholars of Dutch learning he read and consulted, Kazan was unable to isolate China or even East Asia. His *Gaikoku jijōsho* ruminated on the way in which the five great religions of the world—Confucianism, Buddhism, Islam, Judaism, and Christianity—had originated in the teachings of the East. Of their founders, only Confucius had lived north of the thirtieth parallel. But in case after case those creeds, as they were brought north to less-developed peoples, had been appropriated and changed, ending up in the hands of barbarian conquerors. His three most important examples were Turkey for Islam, Europe for Christianity and Judaism, and Manchu China for Confucianism. Of these both the West and China now posed problems for Japan, though it was already clear that the threat from the West was the greater.[34]

The political economist Satō Nobuhiro (1769–1850) was absorbed in many of the intellectual currents of his day. He studied successively astronomy, geography, surveying, and

33. *Hayashi Shihei zenshū* (Tokyo, 1943), pp. 114–115.
34. Satō Shōsuke, *Yōgakushi kenkyū josetsu* (Tokyo, 1980), pp. 159–160.

Confucianism; traveling widely, he was the author of works on prices, management, and government. In his forties he became aware of Western encroachments on Asia and began to concern himself with problems of national defense, for which he wrote treatises on land and naval warfare. He is known for the combination of nationalism, rationalist political economy, and administrative planning that distinguished much late Edo statecraft. Status divisions in society were to be replaced in a sweeping reorganization that would produce a corporate state in control of productive forces. In his *Kaibō-saku,* dating from the turn of the century, he surveyed Japan's possible enemies. England's strength related to its commerce, Russia's to its size; but Japan had a more formidable problem close at hand. "The great country of Ch'ing is vast," he wrote, "and if a crafty king should arise and do his worst, the misery this could bring us would be greater than any Russia could inflict." Consequently he thought it desirable that Japan cultivate China through trade and friendship.[35] A decade later, after he had absorbed the influence of Hirata Atsutane kokugaku, his opinions changed. In 1823 he wrote "A Secret Plan for Confusing Times" (*Kondō hisaku*). Now the peerless polity of Japan was surrounded by corrupt barbarian peoples; it was Japan's mission to subdue them and unify the world. Conquest should begin where it would be easiest, and that was across the Yellow Sea. "Of all the countries in the world", Satō wrote, "the place we can most easily take is Manchuria, which we can seize from China (Shina). It is some eight hundred *ri* from our northern territories, and it will not be difficult for us to take advantage of China's decline." Disorder, he thought, was increasing, and the Ch'ing government was distracted by its border problems. The Chinese were in

35. *Kaibō saku,* in *Satō Nobuhiro kagaku zenshū* (Tokyo, 1927), vol. 3, p. 823.

any case weak and cowardly, and the masses would panic at the sight of Japanese forces.[36]

Sentiments like these bridge *The Battles of Coxinga* and the rhetoric of a Shōwa politician like Mori Kaku, who lost no opportunity to disparage China. Satō's writing still has a setting of fantasy and speculation, and he was holding out his vision of a mighty Japan with all countries under its direction as a stimulus for the massive social and economic realignment he thought desirable for Japan itself. Those plans—a great imperial capital in the Kantō and regional centers throughout Japan, return of warriors to the countryside, and a new sort of command economy—seemed sufficiently prescient in the early Shōwa period to guarantee their author a great deal of attention, attention he lost just as quickly after Japan's defeat in World War II.

What matters, however, is this: as the difficulties of facing an apparently irresistible and dynamic West confronted Japan in the middle decades of the nineteenth century, attitudes that reflected in varying degrees the Japan-centered thought of Tokugawa writers, realistic evaluations of alternatives worked out by students of Western learning, romantic dreams of future national greatness, and awareness of China's weakness in the face of the Western challenge—all these forces combined to bring Japanese to see China in a new light.

36. *Kondo hisaku,* in Takimoto Seiichi, ed., *Nihon keizai taiten* (Tokyo, 1929), vol. 18, pp. 567–631.

3 The Meiji Aftermath

IN THE MIDDLE OF the nineteenth century, Japan's relative isolation from Asian and world currents suddenly gave way to active participation in regional and world politics and trade. The stable societies of China and Korea, which had constituted a defensive barrier protecting Japan from the warlike horsemen of Central Asia, could not protect it from the seaborne challenge of the West. In a remarkably short period of time, Japan was to repay, as Irokawa Daikichi puts it, "neighborly friendship with enmity" and with action quite "contrary to the teachings . . . of the Buddha and of Confucius, even though the Japanese themselves had revered them as spiritual teachers."[1] Some of what has gone before suggests that this may not have been as abrupt a switch of attitude as one might think. Nevertheless, the bearing of the modern Japanese imperial state toward Asia transformed regional and world politics.

The transition from Tokugawa to Meiji attitudes toward China was neither simple nor sudden. Tokugawa scholars had long thought of Chinese civilization as their own, as we have seen, and they distinguished between the land of the Sages that they studied and the country ruled by Manchus

1. *The Culture of the Meiji Period*, p. 4.

that they could not visit. In Meiji years they were able to travel there. In late Tokugawa times books from China had brought warnings of the danger from the West. They also brought Chinese translations of Western works on politics, history, and international law done in the treaty ports along the China coast, and these were avidly studied in Japan. This process remains little studied because it was so short in duration, but it was of considerable significance in the 1860s and 1870s.

On the other hand, most commoners during the centuries of Tokugawa seclusion were only vaguely aware of foreign countries as some kind of outsider or others, which was generally assumed to be Chinese. The street crowds who hailed or hooted at any non-Japanese as "Tōjin!" were conscious chiefly of dress and appearance. A generation or two later, their descendants were more specific in their derision of Chinese on the streets as "chan chan bōzu!," but they too were not expressing very new or different evaluations. Nevertheless it is clear that in the overall relationship between Japan and China something new was at work, something that made it easy to vaunt Japan as superior to Asia in general and China in particular. It remains to sketch out some of the elements that went into the new image.

Restoration Rhetoric

In recent writing one finds a new balance between new and old, rational and irrational, in discussions of the cultural policies pursued by the fledgling Meiji state after its establishment in 1868. Its pronouncements of "restoration" carried with them a series of institutional changes that were innovative and indeed revolutionary in their consequences, but they were couched in language and accompanied by rites that invoked the kokugaku affirmations of antiquity, an antiquity that was part rediscovery and part invention. Ministries of Rites and of Doctrine mobilized thousands of propagandists for the dissemination of new national teachings and the proscription of Buddhism. The initial intensity of this drive subsided after the early years. Pragmatic bureaucrats recognized that the Shinto ideologues had mounted a drive for political power and blocked it. Chastened Buddhists were readmitted to the nationalist fold and politely pretended that they had never been persecuted, and with the Iwakura embassy to the Western World of 1871–1873 the core leadership turned decisively to the West in its search for institutional models. Still the vaulting arrogance of the early days was never formally renounced but was in fact incorporated in many of the new institutions, with the result that education and socialization for civil and military service made it part of the mental conditioning of the Japanese masses.[2] In their long-term consequences the early pronouncements can be made to seem, and were, far-sighted, rational, and innovative. But in their context and time, the panoply of engineered antiquity that was held over them also made them seem archaic.

It is, I think, true that over time this affirmation of indigenous excellence made a significant contribution to views of the "other" as less worthy and less important, and that this contributed to the bland self-assurance with which imperial Japan regarded its neighbors on the continent. A land in possession of the perfect polity could show no greater kindness than to enfold others in that polity. The infuriating (to those others) arrogance of imperial rescripts that extended Japan's

2. I refer particularly to Martin Collcutt, "Buddhism: The Threat of Eradication," in Marius B. Jansen and Gilbert Rozman, eds., *Japan in Transition: From Tokugawa to Meiji* (Princeton: Princeton University Press, 1986); Helen Hardacre, *Shintō and the State, 1868–1988* (Princeton: Princeton University Press, 1989); and James Edward Ketelaar, *Of Heretics and Martyrs in Meiji Japan: Buddhism and Its Persecution* (Princeton: Princeton University Press, 1990).

governance to Koreans and others fortunate enough to come under the imperial sway surely owed something to the new parochialism that claimed to be heir to a mythic antiquity.

And yet one has to guard against taking refuge in the comfortable confines of denouncing the "emperor system" (*tennōsei*), criticism that has sometimes served as a substitute for analysis in a good deal of postwar writing in Japan. These ideas grew so well because the soil in society and thought was prepared for them, and we have noted that preparation in some areas of the Tokugawa world. The rhetoric of imperial restoration did have internal dynamics that strengthened these themes, but it was far from the whole story.

Practical Problems, Tactics, and Perceptions

The major factor in Japan's change of posture toward China was the question of priorities in its recovery of sovereignty in the revision of the unequal treaties that the shogunate had negotiated with the powers in the 1850s and 1860s. The problem centered on the most-favored-nation clause, whereby general approval by all the foreign powers was required before privileges granted to any of them could be reclaimed. Tariff autonomy and extraterritorial rights could not be negotiated piecemeal. When the Meiji government came to power, many of its leaders optimistically assumed that a reform government would be able to negotiate anew, and certainly after 1872 when the treaties were scheduled for renewal or renegotiation. The discovery that this was not the case called into question the facile hopes that had been placed in the efficacy of international law to correct injustice between nations. It seemed to call for a new realism.

In this context Japan's relations with its neighbors clearly had to be viewed in the larger context of how they would affect Japan's relations with the Western powers. Conceivably, two approaches to China might have been taken: cooperation or competition. At the outset there were many voices raised in favor of cooperation. Late Tokugawa advocates of opening, among them Katsu Kaishū, had often phrased their arguments in terms of a possible mission for Japan as leader of the countries of East Asia against further Western incursions.[3] Upon closer examination, however, the argument was not very convincing. Leaders require followers, and there was not much reason to expect Korea, much less China, to follow Japan's lead. The early Tokugawa shoguns had abandoned any thought of participation in a Chinese world order because they could not do so on a basis of equality, and nineteenth-century Chinese leaders were no more likely to change their position in this regard than their seventeenth-century predecessors had been. Japanese government leaders had additional problems with the idea of cooperation. Success ultimately depended on the approval of the Western powers that controlled international affairs in the nineteenth century, and China's disastrous course of foreign war and internal rebellion did not make the Meiji leaders eager to seem allied with a loser. And so competition rather quickly replaced cooperation as a tactic.

This was probably inevitable, for the reports and impressions that early Japanese travelers to China and the West brought back with them, added to the intelligence received from other sources, fixed a negative perception of contemporary China in Japanese minds. The first official embassy to the outer world was a mission sent to Washington to exchange signatures for the treaty negotiated by Townsend Harris. In 1860 three bakufu officials led an entourage of seventy-six men to Washington. Of the several diaries the officials kept,

---

3. Marius B. Jansen, *Sakamoto Ryōma and the Meiji Restoration* (Princeton: Princeton University Press, 1961), p. 165.

one, that of Vice-Ambassador Muragaki, Awaji no kami No-
rimasa, *Kōkai nikki,* serves to illustrate their awareness of
the significance of the journey. "In olden days," he recorded
on learning of his assignment, "envoys were dispatched to
China, but that is only a neighboring country across a strip of
water. The United States, however, is more than 10,000 *ri*
away from Japan, and when it is day in that country it is night
in ours." Thus a consciousness of a shift in the designation of
models was there at the beginning. The envoys exchanged
formal poems among themselves in Chinese to commemorate
the importance of their task.

Throughout the visits to Washington and New York, they
marveled at strange customs and sights—but with little desire
to participate in what they saw. Their attention was fixed on
the need to maintain their dignity as representatives of Japan.
Confident that the curiosity their visit aroused was evidence
of success in this task, Muragaki allowed himself a conde-
scending *waka* that remarked on his willingness to "allow
barbarians to gaze upon the bright glory of the Eastern Land
of the Rising Sun." Nothing he saw suggested that there was
a great deal to learn in the West. On being shown shriveled
heads in the anthropological collection of the Smithsonian,
his distaste was barely concealed as he noted, "It is no accident that we call these people barbarians."

On the other hand, there were things to learn about matters
of cultural priority; the Japanese, it seemed, had made some
curious choices in the past. As the embassy ship returned by
way of the Atlantic and Indian oceans to complete its circum-
navigation of the globe, it coaled at Luanda in West Africa.
Muragaki wrote that the Africans he saw in port seemed to
resemble apes; the sounds they made were like the croak of
frogs, and their hair, "frizzled to its roots, did not grow at all,
but remained short like the hair we often see on the heads of
our Buddhist images." They looked, he thought, "invariably

like the very image of Dharma, walked barefoot, and squatted on the ground in the manner of a primitive tribe." In fact, he decided, "the natives of India and of Africa both belong to one and the same tribe, of whom that Buddha must have been a chieftain. If so, how absurd it is to worship Buddha or Amitabha at our altars! Even more absurd, that our priests shave their heads in imitation of these natives' frizzled hair, wear a surplice of gold brocade in the same way these natives cover themselves with shawl-like cloths, and carry their bowl of offering in the same manner that these natives use coconut cups to eat their food!" Clearly the early Meiji anti-Buddhist rage did not spring entirely from Shinto-centered imperial loyalism.

As the ship entered Hong Kong, the party felt that it was almost home, and the ambassadors' poems began to yearn more strongly for Japan. But now they ruminated on the fate of China. The Manchu regime was in the throes of its second round of warfare with the European powers; much of Canton had been burned, the Hsien-feng emperor had fled Peking, and the capital had fallen to the allied forces. "What a sad history," Muragaki noted, "and what a fearful lesson it teaches us! . . . The Chinese, we have learned, are poor soldiers, and it was the Mongols who put up a stiff resistance. Even within China itself uprisings are taking place as rebels recruit volunteers under the slogan of restoring the Ming Dynasty once more . . . This is the unfortunate lot of China, once the proud empire that held sway over more than 400 *hsien*." [4]

We should not make too much of this. A contemporary commentator noted that Muragaki, at forty-seven the oldest

---

4. I have adapted the translation of the diary by Helen Uno issued as *Kōkai Nikki: The Diary of the First Japanese Embassy to the United States of America* (Tokyo, 1958). The embassy is the subject of Masao Miyoshi, *As We Saw Them: The First Japanese Embassy to the United States* (Berkeley: University of California Press, 1979), which examines all the diaries in a study of the mind-set of the ambassadors.

of the three principal ambassadors, "was so great a sufferer from sea-sickness during the passage to Honolulu that he never appeared on deck, and was even confined to his berth in the lower cabin the greater part of the time . . . He seemed attached to the Embassy merely as a makeweight, and it was never observed that he was consulted respecting any of their movements, or volunteered any suggestions on the subjects presented to their consideration."[5] Still the mission and future trips like it left enduring impressions on young travelers who were more involved and more intelligent than Muragaki, men whose responses proved more representative of their peers. Fukuzawa Yukichi, the future educator, writer, and publisher, and Fukuchi Genichirō, who was, like Fukuzawa, to travel on future missions to the West, left no doubt in their writings and lives that they were fully aware of the critical importance of what they were seeing. But it is also true that for some of them, certainly for Fukuzawa, the awareness that Japan faced a turning point in its search for models and examples had come before their ship left Yokohama.

Additional travel and first-hand impressions that Japanese formed as they entered international society reinforced these tendencies. The relevance of China's experience of defeat and humiliation was obvious to everyone in Japan who thought about it. Nineteenth-century commentators provided a variety of emphases, but they were united in warning that while the events they recorded might be taking place in a neighboring country, they also applied directly to Japan. Satō Nobuhiro, whose ideas of expansion and reorganization were mentioned earlier, was influential in the policies worked out by the chief bakufu minister Mizuno Tadakuni in the 1840s. It was not enough to fortify Edo Bay with guns as the government was doing, he warned; Japan needed ships to keep the

5. Appendix to *Kōkai Nikki*, from *China and Japan* by Lieutenant James L. Johnston, U.S.N. (Philadelphia, 1860).

enemy out of its coastal waters. The urgency of the situation also influenced his organization policies. The wealth of the country had ended up in the hands of great merchants, and the only way to recover it for national purposes was to institute policies of central control through state enterprise. Yokoi Shōnan, in writing his "Three Policies for the Country" in 1860, noted that Japan's fate was bound to that of China, and he deplored Chinese obscurantism that tried to classify the Western barbarians with birds and beasts. It was up to Japan to adopt realistic mercantile policies, to learn from Western foreigners, and to speed steps for building a navy. Then came tidings of the Taiping rebellion, with its reminder of the subversive potential of Christianity. The true dimensions of the classic Chinese formulation of "Troubles from without, Disaster from within" (*Naiyū-gaikan*) were now apparent.

In 1862 the Chōshū samurai leader Takasugi Shinsaku visited Shanghai for two months. His diary is replete with warnings of the significance of China's shameful weakness in the face of Western power and details of the humiliation regularly inflicted on Chinese by Westerners. "When British and French walk along the street, Chinese move aside and get out of their way. Shanghai is Chinese territory, but it really belongs to the British and the French . . . This is bound to happen to us too." His notations added details of the destruction and loss of life incurred in the Taiping suppression. There was, as Haga Noboru points out, little empathy for the Chinese in his writing, but instead the notion that China's distress was fortunately buying some time for Japan. His astonishment at the contrast between the formidable buildings for foreigners and the conditions of poverty and filth for the Chinese, and his implied warnings about missionary tactics infiltrating through such charitable works as hospitals, put one in mind of the warnings of Aizawa Seishisai decades earlier. Small wonder that Takasugi and his Chōshū colleagues, as well as their martyred teacher Yoshida Shōin, who wrote of these matters from prison, rejoiced in news of the Taiping suppression.[6]

And so competition rather quickly replaced cooperation. China was not, in any case, interested in cooperation and preferred to seek Western help against Japan in policies traditionally described as "using barbarians to control barbarians." Tokyo in turn was quick to use the proximity and apparent weakness of China for its own internal and external purposes.

When the Meiji government sought to reduce samurai restlessness in 1874 by substituting a maritime adventure for the proposed chastisement of Korea, its target was the island of Taiwan, where aborigines had attacked Okinawan sailors. The forceful diplomacy of Ōkubo Toshimichi would have resulted in war, if the Ch'ing court had not reversed its stand and agreed to pay an indemnity. The Chōshū leader Kido Takayoshi, convinced that Ōkubo's tactics were leading Japan into an unnecessary war that could only serve to delay the progress of social and political reforms, resigned his offices, convinced, as he wrote in his diary, that "the national treasury will be emptied overnight, a great disparity will develop between the value of gold and paper money, and disorder will arise through the land." But he also abandoned hope of peace because, "though it is regrettable, nothing can be done."[7] Thus presumably the outbreak of violence would have brought him around, despite his opposition to the policies that led to it.

6. See the richly documented discussion by Haga Noboru, "Chūgoku to teikoku-shugi: Ahen sensō, Taihei tengoku, Nihon," in the festschrift for Tanaka Masayoshi, *Chūgoku kindaishi no shomondai—Tanaka Masayoshi Sensei kinen rombunshū* (Tokyo, 1984). I am grateful to Joshua Fogel for calling this to my attention. See also Etō Shinkichi, "Nihonjin no Chūgokukan—Takasugi Shinsaku ra no baai," in *Nihon to Ajiya-Niida Noboru Hakushi tsuitō rombunshū*, vol. 3 (Tokyo, 1970), and Ichiko Chūzō, "Bakumatsu Nihonjin no Taihei tengoku ni kansuru chishiki," in *Kindai Chūgoku no seiji to shakai* (Tokyo, 1971).

7. *The Diary of Kido Takayoshi*, vol. 3, trans. Sidney Devere Brown and Akiko Hirota (Tokyo, 1986), pp. 83, 93, entries of October 9 and November 1, 1874.

When the Ch'ing leaders followed their successful suppression of the great rebellions that almost toppled the dynasty with military and naval reforms on the Western model, the Meiji military leaders began to see China as a possible opponent. The future prime minister and prince, Katsura Tarō, was ordered to survey Chinese military capabilities in 1879, went secretly to China himself, and assigned ten officers to travel throughout the country to make military surveys. The result of this investigation, issued with a foreword by Yamagata Aritomo, was put out in 1880 and revised in 1882 and 1889. Yamagata's foreword noted that China was no more the country of yesterday than Japan was; the Chinese were employing foreign military advisers and purchasing weapons from England and Germany; in view of the world situation in which imperialist nations like Russia operated in total disregard for international law, it was incumbent upon Japan to inform itself thoroughly. The result was a meticulous accounting of Chinese banner forces and regular troops, their dispositions, bases, organization, weapons, and strength.[8]

Although cooperation as a possibility was abandoned by Meiji leaders, it lived on in the ideas of intellectuals and activists outside the establishment. Ōi Kentarō, a leading figure in the Jiyū-minken (People's Rights) movement of the 1880s, for instance, worked to organize a filibustering expedition to Korea (which proved abortive) to speed reform there, hoping that its success would serve to accelerate the movement toward democracy in Japan. One of his companions, Tarui Tōkichi, did his best to work with revolutionaries in both Korea and Hong Kong to "revive" Asia. He wrote a slim volume in the 1880s advocating union with Korea; it was confiscated during his imprisonment for activities relating to the banned socialist organization Tōyō shakaitō. Rewritten after his release, *Nikkan gappō ron* advocated a union of Japan and Ko-

8. "Military Preparedness of Neighboring Countries" (*Rimpō heibi ryaku*), microfilm.

rea with the argument that neither country had any hope of maintaining its independence alone against the predatory West and that, just as European countries and the United States represented unions of earlier political entities, East Asian survival would require the construction of a state sufficiently large and strong to withstand the West.[9]

Government leaders, however, were not tempted by such ideas, which were usually the product of people on the fringe of political responsibility. Tarui, for one, had been enthusiastic about Saigō Takamori's Satsuma rebellion, then joined with Ōi Kentarō in the Osaka incident, and later became involved with an educational institute in Shanghai and movements for Mongolian independence before he stood successfully for election for the House of Representatives in 1892. There he once again worked with Ōi to establish an organization they called the East Asian Liberal Party. But seasoned politicians, even one as favorably inclined toward such activities as the Saga parliamentarian Soejima Taneomi (1828–1905), tended to give such ideas short shrift. When one of the "Asianists," Ura Keiichi, approached Soejima in 1885 to explain his hopes for Japanese union with Korea and possibly even China, he heard his ideas ridiculed as "student nonsense." "What kind of world do you think this is?" Soejima asked, and went on to answer his own question:

> It's a world in which strong countries annex weak countries, develop them and make them serve their purposes, and fight over them. To live in a world of struggle like this we have to build up our military strength. Nobody without military power can stand in a world like this . . . The only way for Japan to preserve its independence for the long future is to acquire territory on the mainland.

9. Reprinted in Takeuchi Yoshimi, ed., *Ajiya shugi, Gendai Nihon shisō taikei* (Tokyo, 1963), pp. 106–129.

And the only territory it can get on the mainland is in Korea and China. You students can prattle on about justice and Western culture . . . But it's different for responsible political leaders like us. To wage war in order to make one's country strong is the highest justice and loyalty to country and ruler.[10]

By 1885 these were becoming familiar contentions. Satō Nobuhiro, we noted, had argued for China's eastern provinces in Manchuria as the only territory Japan could seize, and a number of individuals in Restoration days had, like Tarui Tōkichi a few decades later, cruised coastal waters of Korea hoping wistfully to find some uninhabited islands. Still Soejima's direct equation of independence with expansion, and expansion with Korea and China, put the matter with particular bluntness.

Others, less inclined toward expansion, nevertheless concluded that Japan's association with Asian neighbors could only slow its march toward equality with the Western powers. Fukuzawa Yukichi, a student of Western learning and youthful interpreter on the Muragaki mission to the United States in 1860, had assumed formidable stature by the mid-1880s as a transmitter of Western ideas, educator, and publicist. He had tried, and failed, to influence reform in Korea by providing education for Korean students at Keiō and showing friendship and support for Korean reformers. But after pro-Japanese groups failed in their attempt to take over the direction of government policy in Seoul in 1884, and as the French victory in Indo-China pointed to the further increase of European power in Asia, Fukuzawa turned his back on the idea of providing aid and comfort to reform forces in Asia. In

10. Quoted in Somura Yasunobu, "Tairiku seisaku ni okeru *imeeji* no tenkai," in Shinohara Hajime and Mitani Taiichirō, eds., *Kindai Nihon no seiji shidō: Seijika kenkyū II* (Tokyo, 1965), pp. 256–257.

March 1885 he editorialized in *Jiji shimpō* that Japan should "part with Asia." It was hopeless to expect recalcitrant obscurantists on the continent to opt for progress, and it was unwise to appear to side with them. "If we keep bad company," he concluded, "we cannot avoid getting a bad name." So clearly what mattered was the perceptions formed in the West; progress for Japan required distancing Japan from Asia.[11]

A few years later in 1887, when Inoue Kaoru resigned his post as foreign minister, he gave authoritative backing for such arguments in a memorandum he sent his colleagues. Everywhere in Asia, he noted, European powers were getting stronger. Their power was constantly augmented by their ability to exploit the colonies they were taking under their control. It seemed to him that China and Japan were probably the only countries that retained even a small hope of maintaining their independence. Consequently the Japanese had to act like the Europeans. "What we have to do," Inoue wrote, "is transform our empire and our people, make the empire like the countries of Europe and our people like the peoples of Europe. To put it differently, we have to establish a new, European-style empire on the edge of Asia."[12] It will be agreed that such conclusions left little room for cooperation with Japan's Asian neighbors.

There remained some who disagreed. Realists considered them dreamers. But as the institutional framework of the Meiji state took final form in the late 1880s and early 1890s, a number of interesting nonconformists turned their backs on

11. "Datsu-A ron," the editorial in question, appears in *Fukuzawa Yukichi zenshū* (Tokyo, 1960), vol. 10, pp. 238–240. See Kenneth Pyle's discussion of the essay in *The New Generation in Meiji Japan: Problems of Cultural Identity, 1885–1895* (Stanford: Stanford University Press, 1969), p. 149.

12. *Segai Inoue Kō den,* vol. 3 (Tokyo, 1936), pp. 907–937.

the established route to success in society and politics and did their best to recapture an Asian identity that seemed in danger of being lost. A loose-knit group, these liberally inclined real-ists talked about and worked for the "regeneration of Asia" in company with would-be reformers from other countries who found themselves in Japan. Unfortunately they had little to offer them except personal commitment and contacts with other groups, often on the political right, who sometimes had different aims in mind. Despite their talk of oriental morality and common cause, they risked misdirecting their Asian friends and helping the Japanese expansionists. [13]

Meiji Sinologues and China

What of the Japanese Confucianists, life-long students of Chi-nese culture and classics, who now found it possible to travel to a country that their predecessors had been able to see only in the elaborate "borrowed scenery" of daimyo gardens? I noted earlier how welcome the opportunity to contact real Chinese in the new mission established in Tokyo was for aris-tocratic scholar-aesthetes like Ōkōchi Teruna, the former daimyo of Takasaki, who found it a pleasant retreat from the realities of a program of forced modernization. We saw also that the premier sinologues of eighteenth-century Japan had been able to separate the classical China of their scholarship and the contemporary country ruled by invaders from north of the Wall. It is therefore not surprising that Meiji sinologues who went to China at a time when it was struggling against internal disruption and imperialist pressures became, if any-

13. See the autobiography of Miyazaki Tōten, *My Thirty-Three Years' Dream,* trans. Etō Shinkichi and Marius B. Jansen (Princeton: Princeton University Press, 1982), and Marius B. Jansen, *The Japanese and Sun Yat-sen* (Cambridge: Harvard University Press, 1954).

thing, more conscious of their Japanese identity. Not for them was Ogyū Sorai's characterization of himself as an "Eastern barbarian."

Takeuchi Minoru's and Joshua Fogel's examinations of the diaries of several leading sinologues who traveled in China open new avenues for study. Takezoe Shin'ichirō (1842–1917), a scholar-diplomat from Kumamoto, first went to China as assistant to Mori Arinori in 1875–76. In 1879 he published his account of 111 days of travel undertaken in 1876. His values were still firmly Confucian, and his travel account, written in elegant Chinese, reflects his gratification at having finally arrived in the homeland of culture. He spent numerous evenings with Chinese literati, exchanging poems and establishing his own identity as a scholar. Takezoe recognized several problems in the Chinese polity but expressed his confidence that the self-strengthening movements then in progress would overcome these difficulties. Yet Takezoe was also a realpolitik diplomat. Later he proposed, from a consular post at Tientsin, steps to take advantage of the Sino-Russian confrontation at Ili, and in his next post, at Seoul, he bore major responsibility for Japanese participation in the abortive plot of 1884. Upon the resolution of those events, he retired to academic work of considerable importance for which he was rewarded with the distinctions of a doctorate and membership in the Imperial Academy.[14]

Oka Senjin's lifespan (1833–1914) extended from education at the Tokugawa Shōheikō Academy, where he studied with such major Confucian scholars as Satō Issai, to the eve of World War I. He was a participant in Restoration politics (and incarcerated for that by his lord) and became a teacher and librarian in Tokyo who taught some three thousand stu-

14. Takeuchi Minoru, "Meiji Kangakusha no Chūgoku kikō," in *Nihonjin ni totte no Chūgokuzō* (Tokyo, 1966), and the biography by Kawamura Ichio in *Kokushi daijiten* (Tokyo, 1988), vol. 9, p. 119.

dents. He went to China in 1884, the year before Fukuzawa's famous editorial, and stayed for almost a year. His account, written in *kanbun* though less elegant in literary style than Takezoe's effort, was published in 1892. If Fukuzawa had argued the general case for separation from Asia, Oka's account provided the documentation for the argument. What he pictured was a country and society in decay. That this picture should be drawn by a man who was perhaps the most prominent sinologue of his time was of profound significance. China, he decided, was afflicted by two poisons. The first was opium. Oka's discovery of the prevalence of this affliction began with this astonishment that the prominent intellectual Wang T'ao was "indisposed" because of his habit when Oka first tried to visit him. His account was replete with descriptions of the casual attitude toward addiction that he encountered. The second poison was addiction to the classics. Seeing extended families comprising sixty or seventy people, with their immense wastefulness and inefficiency, gave him a new awareness of familism in the name of filiality, and innumerable written conversations with upper-class Chinese convinced him of their obscurantism and cultural conservatism. His arguments that the Way of the Sages in contemporary times should involve reform and reconstruction fell on deaf ears. Oka's negative readings were the more powerful because they came from a man for whom the Confucian past had been vitally important; he now concluded that Japan should separate itself from that heritage.[15]

From then on, every sinologue went to China. Their travelogues provide important material for the understanding of

15. Takeuchi, pp. 249–264. Discussed also with other aspects of Meiji views in Marius B. Jansen, "Japanese Views of China During the Meiji Period," in Albert Feuerwerker, Rhoads Murphey, and Mary C. Wright, eds., *Approaches to Modern Chinese History* (Berkeley: University of California Press, 1967), and Joshua Fogel, "Confucian Pilgrim: Uno Tetsuto's Travels in China" (manuscript).

late nineteenth- and twentieth-century Japanese views and policy. The popular works of the prominent Kyoto scholar Naitō Konan, especially his treatise on China, *Shina ron* (1914), provided powerful and authoritative support for the view that the key element in Chinese society was localism, and that the integrative forces behind the great dynastic periods of strong political organization were no longer able to overcome the disintegrative pressures of family and region.[16] Far from providing support for the traditional admiration of Chinese society and civilization, then, leading sinologues' contribution can be seen as reinforcing attitudes articulated by practitioners of realpolitik who found it essential for Japan to separate itself openly from nineteenth-century China.

War with China and Equality with the West

In 1894 Japan achieved treaty equality with the West, defeated the armies and sank the navy of Ch'ing China, and promptly joined the circle of imperialist powers in 1895 by securing at Shimonoseki all that it had objected to in the unequal treaties with which the Western powers had saddled the late Tokugawa government. Indeed, it secured more: its efforts to claim the Liaotung peninsula were thwarted by the triple intervention of France, Germany, and Russia, but Taiwan was ceded to Japan, more treaty ports were established, and additional clauses that provided for the right to build manufacturing facilities in treaty ports located in foreign settlements, protected by extraterritoriality, made Japan the benefactor of the other imperialist powers. Thus in only a

16. Yue-him Tam, "An Intellectual's Response to Western Intrusion: Naitō Konan's View of Republican China," in Akira Iriye, ed., *The Chinese and the Japanese: Essays in Political and Cultural Interactions* (Princeton: Princeton University Prees, 1980), and Joshua Fogel, *Politics and Sinology: The Case of Naitō Konan, 1866–1934* (Cambridge: Harvard University Press, 1984).

decade the advice of Fukuzawa to "part with Asia" and the determination of Inoue to "build a Western-style empire on the edge of Asia" had come to fruition. This marked the beginning of policies that Irokawa deplored as repaying good with evil.

It did not seem that way to many contemporaries. The maladroit performance of the Ch'ing military forces seemed symptomatic of the decay of the Chinese imperial system. Fukuzawa Yukichi had editorialized on the outbreak of war: "We intend only to develop world civilization and to defeat those who obstruct it . . . this is not a war between people and people and country and country, but a kind of religious war." Uchimura Kanzō, a Christian leader who had stood almost alone in resisting the ideological claims of the emperor system, wrote that since Japan's announced purpose to liberate Korea from Chinese suzerainty was unselfish and pure, it was reasonable to see it as a just war. "Japan's victory," he wrote, "will mean free government, free religion, free education, and free commerce for 600 million souls that live on this side of the globe." For the journalist Tokutomi Sohō, tired of a life lived in the shadow of Western power, "the true nature of our country, our national character, will emerge like the sun breaking through a dense fog." [17]

The euphoria did not last very long. Fukuzawa was content to see his country emerge as a regional power, but Uchimura rued his enthusiasm when he learned of the terms of peace, concluded it had been a "piratical war," and thereafter adopted a pacifist position. Tokutomi, for his part, was so outraged by Japan's inability to retain Liaotung that he spent the rest of his long career campaigning for greater national strength. Most Japanese accepted his argument that the costs, however heavy, of additional divisions and additional battle-

17. Discussed in Marius B. Jansen, *Japan and China: From War to Peace, 1894–1972* (Chicago: Rand McNally, 1975), p. 47.

ships were the inevitable price of national greatness. Since Japan's exposure of China's weakness brought on a new round of demands and seemed almost to precipitate the breakup of China, Japan was soon struggling to achieve a major share and a special position. The Western powers, it could be argued, had already achieved their needs in other areas. Japan's costs in men and treasure, particularly in the war with Russia in 1904–05 that led to the retention of Liaotung and the annexation of Korea, had been far heavier than those of the Western powers; continental Asia was far closer and more important to Japan than it was to its frequently hypocritical critics. So direct criticism of expansion was relatively rare, although the tactics and arrogance of the military who were in its vanguard were not always popular. Their posture as the agents of the emperor's will, however, muted criticism in times of crisis.

All this is common knowledge. Does it deserve the laments so often heard in postwar Japan, that this was a remarkably ungrateful return for cultural benefits so freely gained from Chinese culture? Let us look again at arguments advanced by Ogyū Sorai in the eighteenth century, to the effect that the true wisdom of the Sages had been abandoned in the land that gave it birth and that, even as an Eastern barbarian, he might well be closer to the truth than his counterparts on the mainland. In Meiji days Naitō Konan modernized this approach. Influenced by the historian Uchida Ginzō, who traced the flow of Western civilization from the eastern Mediterranean to Greece and Rome and then to Western Europe, Naitō discerned a similar course in East Asia, where the classical culture of the Yellow River basin had moved south to the Yangtze basin and crossed the China Sea to Japan, where it found fertile soil in a setting that provided ancillary strengths of organization and direction. The political entity of China, under Manchu rule, had devolved into regional and familial

localism and paid only lip service to the Way of the Sages.
China, as Oka Senjin put it, was caught in an addiction to the
classical past, coupled with its addiction to self-gratification
through opium.

To extend the argument a step further, the flow of Chinese
and Korean ceramics, art, and other treasures to Japan could
be seen as evidence of taste and appreciation by purchasers
who were rescuing them from possible destruction. Surely
one need not make moral distinctions between Yamagata
Aritomo, Idemitsu Sazō, and other connoisseurs who enriched the gardens and museums of twentieth-century Japan
and the Earl of Elgin and his generation, who stripped the
Parthenon of its marble friezes and ransacked the ancient
world for appropriate curios for their homes and gardens.
The Englishmen had grown up with Homer, Hesiod, Ovid,
and Virgil; most of them prided themselves on an amateur
ability in classic verse and counted their civilization as heir to
everything good that had gone before. Some, like Lord Byron,
even threw themselves into political action designed to "save"
the ancient world, in somewhat the way that Meiji dreamers
thought they could make a difference in Korea and China.

To say that the Japanese situation was not nearly so unique
as it has been described is not to praise agents of imperialism,
British or Japanese. China and Korea, moreover, were living
entities with an extraordinary historic continuity and not,
like Greece and Rome, geographical expressions with much
memory but less present. The Meiji Japanese did, however,
have certain explanations that the English lacked. Their country had been pulled into international affairs against its will,
and it was saddled with formidable handicaps. Worse, their
neighbors paid them little heed and seemed to assume that
their long-sustained cultural lag carried over into modern
times as well. Contemporary elites in both China and Korea,
whatever the realities of their institutional makeup, consid-

ered Japan's young samurai government more nuisance than neighbor, until it was too late.

IT MAY BE WELL to end with a word about encounters between members of these political elites. There were many such encounters. Perhaps the most memorable is the long negotiation between Itō Hirobumi and Li Hung-chang at Shimonoseki in 1895, as they worked out the settlement of the war that Japan had won. A more interesting encounter, however, is that between Li Hung-chang and Mori Arinori, when the young Satsuma leader, then only twenty-nine, faced Li, fifty-three, to negotiate Chinese cooperation in Japan's attempt to work out normal treaty relations with Korea.

Li had come to prominence as a commander in the suppression of rebellions in midcentury. In 1870 he was appointed governor-general of the capital province of Chihli and imperial commissioner for the northern ports. In the years that followed, the court relied on him and his forces for defense of the metropolitan area, listened to his suggestions for various steps of "self-strengthening," and used him for a number of diplomatic missions. Tientsin, where he was ordered to develop his headquarters, and Paotingfu were preferred to Peking for negotiations. In 1873 it had fallen to Li to conduct the negotiations with Japan over the initial treaty that put Sino-Japanese relations on a modern basis. Li was the principal official involved in organizing the Chinese response to Japan's expedition to Taiwan in 1874, although the negotiations for its solution were carried out at Peking. By the mid-1870s, then, Li stood out as a strong, relatively modern-minded official, deeply experienced in military and foreign affairs and a bulwark of the Ch'ing court.

Mori Arinori, for his part, had packed an astonishing variety of activities into his short career. Sent to England secretly for study by his domain of Satsuma in the 1860s, he became acquainted with a utopian community movement that took him from England to the United states. When he returned to Japan at the urging of the community's leader, he began his public career with participation in the first institutions designed for representative government. These failing, he entered the foreign service and was appointed first minister to Washington, where he sponsored vigorous studies of American educational institutions. There followed appointment to posts as minister plenipotentiary to China to negotiate with Li, promotion to vice-minister of foreign affairs, minister to Great Britain, and other posts before he took over the ministry of education in 1885, the field in which he most clearly left his mark. Mori had also been, with Fukuzawa, a leading member of the small group of intellectuals who organized the 1873 Society and a journal to speed the process of enlightenment and reform.[18]

The dialogue between Mori and Li thus pitted leading advocates of change in both countries against each other, and the discrepancy in age between them may serve in one sense to symbolize Chinese views of Japan's cultural maturity.

The issue that brought Mori to Tientsin was Japan's continuing difficulty in persuading the Koreans to adopt modern treaty relations. Overtures made in 1868 had been rejected out of hand, and the debate about a response had split the Japanese leadership in 1873 and 1874. In 1875 a Japanese warship's request for food and water had been answered by gunfire, and the Japanese government dispatched Kuroda Kiyotaka and Inoue Kaoru to Korea to demand satisfaction. But since the Korean relationship with China complicated mat-

18. For Li Hung-chang's role at Chihli, see Kwang-ching Liu, "Li Hung-chang in Chihli: The Emergence of a Policy, 1870–1875," in *Approaches to Modern Chinese History*. Mori's career is detailed in Ivan Parker Hall, *Mori Arinori* (Cambridge: Harvard University Press, 1973).

ters, Mori was dispatched to seek Chinese assistance in dealing with Korea. He left Japan late in 1875, but because his ship broke down it required a second attempt before he was able to reach China. After an unproductive encounter with officials of the Tsungli Yamen, he met with Li at Paotingfu on January 25. Their talks were carried on through interpretation into English.[19]

The transcript suggests that Mori began rather awkwardly. He had now been around the world twice, he announced, once departing east to west, once the other way around. What most stayed with him was the feeling he received on shipboard of the deep peace of the boundless ocean. Yes, Li commented, he could imagine that. From such perspectives, Mori went on, the particular differences of countries like Turkey, India, and China were truly astonishing. Li murmured his agreement and asked whether Mori, on the basis of such wide experience and travel, did not have some counsel for him on the proper course of change.

After this preliminary sparring, the two got down to business. Mori complained of Korea's stance, at once independent and subservient to the Chinese order, while Li pointed to Japan's preparedness to use force, both in Korea and more recently in Taiwan. After more debate, Li finally agreed to advise the Tsungli Yamen to approach the Koreans with advice for considering Japanese demands and Mori expressed his thanks.

In a second meeting, after disposing of two or three minor details, Li turned to the subject that leads me to end with their colloquy. Japan's recent policies were on the whole admirable, he thought, but overdone. Why abandon traditional dress for the European fashion? Very simple and hardly

19. I have used the transcript in Japanese in Kimura Tadashi, *Mori Sensei den* (Tokyo, 1889), pp. 86–105. Part of the negotiations is given in English in Ōkubo Toshiaki, ed., *Mori Arinori zenshū*, vol. 1 (Tokyo, 1972), pp. 177–181.

worth discussing, responded Mori; Japan's traditional dress, like that of China, was loose and comfortable but no longer appropriate to the times, which required efficiency and practicality. Li was not convinced. Wasn't the clothing one wore a way of showing respect for one's forebears? No, said Mori, if our ancestors were alive today they would do as we are doing; after all, the Japanese of a millennium earlier had adopted dress like China's when they became familiar with it. And wise they were, countered Li—not only was it appropriate, but all its materials could be produced within Japan; to buy European clothes only drained the country of resources. No, said Mori, Chinese costume might be more comfortable, but it was better suited to indolence than to activity; contemporary Japanese were intent on their business and not interested in being casual; the cost of change today could bring limitless gains in future days. Nonetheless, Li came back: didn't the abandonment of national dress for that of Europe signify a shameful setback for the spirit of national independence? By no means, Mori assured him: Japan's decision for change and reform came from within and was not dictated from abroad. Japan had always taken the best features of other civilizations for its own, and the current readiness to borrow from Asia, America, or wherever was simply a continuation of that tradition. The Chinese, Li replied, had no need to carry out changes as far-reaching as Japan's; they intended merely to take up useful things like military, transportation, and communications technology. But who could predict future needs? asked Mori. Looking, no doubt, at Li's official Manchu robes, he suggested that surely seventeenth-century Chinese had not selected their present costume by choice. Li demurred—at least the Chinese did not have to adopt their dress from Europe. Reform, countered Mori, becoming somewhat testy, is reform. When the Chinese were forced to take such steps, had they not been unpopular? In answer Li, now more Japanese than his guest, assured him piously that it had been done out of loyalty to the emperor. Then, tiring of the issue, Li observed that it seemed probable that everything would depend on future relations between Asia and the Western powers. Would Mori care to give his view of what the probabilities were in that regard?

It was indeed, Mori agreed, a question of overwhelming importance. The world had entered an era of unrelenting competition and struggle between nations. Moreover, while he counted himself an Asian, he thought it undeniable that it would be a matter of some centuries before Asia could compete with Europe on equal terms and that at present most Asian peoples lagged far behind the level of Western development. In what way? asked Li. Mori answered by contrasting Western respect for women with the near contempt he thought Asian peoples had for female intelligence and ability.[20] Did this not prove Asian backwardness? Li was staggered by this argument. Was Mori perhaps a Christian? No, said Mori, he held to no religion, Western, Buddhist, or Islamic, but adopted a course of equality that avoided injustice to anyone. The two ended with agreement to disagree and professions of mutual respect, along with the hope that their countries would fare well in the competition with the Western world.

It may of course be too much to make these two extraordinary individuals stand for whole civilizations. But Mori's practicality and unsentimental willingness to set priorities according to relative advantage and cost surely spoke for the Meiji elite. His irreverent dismissal of tradition, on the other hand, was to cost him his life in 1889, after he offended ultranationalist opinion at the Ise Shrine. He would surely have thought it strange to argue that national policies should be

---

20. Mori's marriage the next month took the form of an equal contract for both parties. Fukuzawa served as witness.

worked out in the light of cultural obligations of the past, the more so when those obligations represented free and independent choices without reference to Chinese participation in or awareness of Japan's cultural borrowing.

Tokugawa participation in the Chinese world was partial, and mutually profitable. It declined in economic and intellectual importance as Japan achieved self-sufficiency and cultural confidence. It left no consciousness of benevolence on the one side and even less sense of obligation on the other.

Bibliographical Note

DESPITE THE IMPORTANCE of the subject for Chinese and Japanese history, writings in Western languages on the relations between Japan and China are surprisingly few. Western historians have understandably given higher priority to the contacts that both countries have had with the West. Thus the travels of Marco Polo to the China of the Mongols brought early and sustained interest, as did that of the Jesuits to China in the Ming and Manchu dynasties. The same was true of Japan, which came to attract the interest of Western writers only after the missionary and commercial contacts of the sixteenth century.

For all practical purposes, study of the relations between Japan and China had to wait until after World War II. Edwin O. Reischauer led the way here. His splendid study of the eighth-century monk Ennin's trip to T'ang China, published as *Ennin's Diary: The Record of a Pilgrimage to China in Search of the Law* (New York: Ronald Press, 1955), was accompanied by *Ennin's Travels in T'ang China* from the same publisher. Important as it was and remains, however, this work essentially relied on its Japanese source for the study of China, although the companion volume placed Ennin's journey solidly within the context of Japanese cultural developments. But it did show the possibilities of approaching Chi-

nese history by way of Japan, and helped to influence my own
efforts in modern history with respect to the contribution that
his Japanese friends made to the work of Sun Yat-sen.
In those beginnings I enjoyed the warm support of both
Reischauer and John K. Fairbank.

Inviting as the vistas were that Reischauer's book held out
for further work, few specialists in early Japanese history followed his example. One who did, with outstanding success,
is Robert Borgen, whose *Sugawara no Michizane and the
Early Heian Court* (Cambridge: Harvard University Press,
1986) is full of fascinating detail about the application of Chinese cultural institutions at the Japanese capital in the ninth
and tenth centuries. Borgen is following this with a study of
the diary of the monk Jōjin, who went to Sung China in 1072
and 1073. Charlotte von Verschuer has also published a valuable account of early relations between China and Japan
through study of the embassies that traveled to China between 702 and 839: *Les Relations officielles du Japon avec la
Chine aux VIIIe et IXe siècles* (Paris: Libraire Droz, 1985).
Her translations from the *Rikkokushi* and careful notation of
monks' itineraries make the book particularly valuable. Earlier Ryusaku Tsunoda and L. Carrington Goodrich made
available accounts of Japan in early Chinese histories: *Japan
in the Chinese Dynastic Histories* (South Pasadena: Perkins,
1951).

In Japanese scholarship, fortunately, this modest harvest is
eclipsed by the work of a number of scholars who devoted
their lives to the study of relations of their country with
China. For the early and medieval period, none contributed
more than the late Mori Katsumi, whose generous assistance
and enthusiastic cooperation provided good counsel for several generations of American students.

Students of Japanese art and Buddhism have made major
contributions to the subject of the cultural impact of China

on Japan in the medieval period, for the interchange of religious visitors never stopped. Among art historians, Yoshiaki Shimizu and James Cahill have done important work, and Martin Collcutt's *Five Mountains: The Rinzai Zen Monastic Institution in Medieval Japan* (Cambridge: Harvard University Press, 1981) is a fine study of the institutional life of monastic Zen. On a more general level, David Pollock's *The Fracture of Meaning: Japan's Synthesis of China from the Eighth through the Eighteenth Centuries* (Princeton: Princeton University Press, 1986) probes the ambivalence of Japanese attitudes toward China by considering how the mix of Chinese and Japanese built into the Japanese writing system worked to define Japan's sense of itself.

Japan's relations with China in medieval times are given general treatment in Kawazoe Shōji's "Japan and East Asia," in Kozo Yamamura, ed., *Cambridge History of Japan*, vol. 3, *Medieval Japan* (Cambridge and New York: Cambridge University Press, 1990), pp. 396–446.

The relations between China and Japan during the almost three centuries of Ming rule are of particular interest. The *wakō*, pirate bands that sailed from islands off the Japanese coast, have drawn particular attention. They are treated in F. W. Mote and Denis Twitchett, eds., *Cambridge History of China*, vol. 7 (Cambridge and New York: Cambridge University Press, 1988), pp. 490–505, and with particular flair by Jurgis Elisonas (George Elison) in John W. Hall, ed., *Cambridge History of Japan*, vol. 4, *Early Modern Japan* (Cambridge and New York: Cambridge University Press, 1991), chap. 6. Tanaka Takeo and Robert Sakai also discuss the issue in a chapter entitled "Japan's Relations with Overseas Countries," in John W. Hall and Toyoda Takeshi, eds., *Japan in the Muromachi Age* (Berkeley: University of California Press, 1977). An earlier account by Wang I-t'ung, *Official Relations between China and Japan, 1368–1549* (Cambridge: Harvard

University Press, 1953), is particularly valuable for the detail
it provides on the frustration experienced by the Ming court
in its efforts to make the Ashikaga shogunate suppress the
pirate bands, and thus illuminates the setting in which trade
and piracy came to flourish in fifteenth- and sixteenth-century
Japan. Also useful is John E. Wills, "Maritime China from
Wang Chih to Shih Lang," in Jonathan D. Spence and John
E. Wills, eds., *From Ming to Ch'ing: Conquest, Region, and
Seventeenth-Century China* (New Haven: Yale University
Press, 1979), which provides more detail on pirate-
adventurers and the Cheng regime on Taiwan.

The reunification of Japan by the armies of Oda Nobunaga, Toyotomi Hideyoshi, and Tokugawa Ieyasu put an end
to offshore disorder only to replace it with the massive invasions Hideyoshi directed against Korea in 1592 and 1597
with the goal of conquering Ming China. The best analysis of
this for Tokugawa statecraft is Ronald P. Toby, *State and Diplomacy in Early Modern Japan: Asia in the Development of
the Tokugawa Bakufu* (Princeton: Princeton University Press,
1984). Toby was the first Western scholar to deprecate the use
of *sakoku* as definitive, pointing out that it derived from a late
Tokugawa translation by Shizuki Tadao of Engelbert Kaempfer's *History of Japan*. He further developed this theme in
"Reopening the Question of *Sakoku*: Diplomacy in the Legitimation of the Tokugawa Bakufu" (1977), as did Kazui
Tashiro in "Foreign Relations during the Edo Period: *Sakoku*
Reexamined" (1982). Both articles appeared in the *Journal of
Japanese Studies*. Tashiro's magisterial work on Tokugawa-
Korean trade, *Kinsei Ni-Chō tsūkō-bōekishi no kenkyū* (To-
kyo, 1981), is of great importance.

In Western scholarship, Japan's importance to China's
needs for precious metal had been indicated by John W. Hall's
discussion of the copper trade in "Notes on the Early Ch'ing
Copper Trade with Japan," *Harvard Journal of Asiatic Stud-*

ies 12 (1949), but broader discussion of currency flows had to wait until the series of studies by William S. Atwell. Built on the work of Kobata Atsushi and others, Atwell's consideration of currency flows in early modern East Asia emphasized the importance of Japanese overseas trade in continental, and indeed world, commerce. Toby and Atwell are editing a set of conference papers for a volume tentatively entitled "International History of Early-Modern East Asia" that promises to become a point of departure for future consideration of these matters. Mention should also be made of the work of European scholars on early modern shipping at the (rather curiously named) Leiden Centre for the History of European Expansion, which is producing a variety of important documentary sources. I have profited particularly from Leonard Blussé's discussion of the Chinese trading diaspora in Southeast Asian commerce and the way that Dutch and Japanese shipping fitted into it, in his *Strange Company: Chinese Settlers, Mestizo Women and the Dutch in VOC Batavia* (Dordrecht, 1986). The subject of Japanese trade with Asia was for many years the special preserve of Iwao Seiichi, and his *Shuinsen bōekishi no kenkyū* (rev. ed., Tokyo, 1985) is a classic.

Nagasaki, its life, governance, and commerce, constitutes a large area of scholarly inquiry. In addition to formal histories and sources for city administration, there are numerous secondary studies. Two stimulating dissertations require mention: Robert LeRoy Innes, "The Door Ajar: Japan's Foreign Trade in the Seventeenth Century" (University of Michigan, 1980), and Aloysius Chang, "The Chinese Community of Nagasaki in the First Century of the Tokugawa Period, 1603–1688" (St. John's University, 1970). I have profited greatly from Nakamura Tadashi, *Kinsei Nagasaki bōekishi no kenkyū* (Tokyo, 1988), and from essays he, Tanaka Takeo, and others provided for the volume issued by the Fukuoka

UNESCO, *Gairai bunka to Kyūshū* (Tokyo, 1973), one of a series of five volumes on Kyushu history. A 1989 conference at the National University of Singapore was the occasion for another valuable set of papers, including pieces by Nakamura and Kamiya Nobuyuki about Tokugawa policy decisions on foreign trade. Mention should also be made of two convenient summaries of the role of Nagasaki: Toyama Mikio, *Nagasaki bugyō: Edo bakufu no mimi to me* (Tokyo, 1988), and Yanai Kenji, *Nagasaki* (Tokyo, 1959). Yamawaki Teijirō, in *Kinsei Ni-Chū bōekishi no kenkyū* (Tokyo, 1960) and *Nagasaki no Tōjin bōeki* (Tokyo, 1964), provides splendid coverage of the Chinese trade at Nagasaki.

The foremost authority on Tokugawa contacts with China is Ōba Osamu of Kansai University. My debt to him is indicated throughout these pages, but those notes cannot do justice to the stimulation he provided during his stay at Princeton in 1981–82. One finds acknowledgment of his influence in many of the writings of Dan Henderson, Ronald Toby, and William Atwell also cited in my notes. Ōba's *Edo jidai ni okeru Tōsen mochiwatarisho no kenkyū* (Kyoto, 1967) is a painstaking study of the import of Chinese books in Tokugawa years. *Edo jidai ni okeru Chūgoku bunka juyō no kenkyū* (Tokyo, 1984) broadens this discussion to culture and culture bearers, and the more general *Edo jidai no Ni-Chū hiwa* (Tokyo, 1980) is a rich source of anecdote. Additional publications provide the texts of reports submitted by arriving ship captains, and much more. For information about Chinese trading ships, see his "Scroll Paintings of Chinese Junks Which Sailed to Nagasaki in the 18th Century and Their Equipment," *The Mariner's Mirror* 60:4 and, for greater detail, "Hirado Mutsuura Shiryō Hakubutsukanzō 'Tōsen no zu' ni tsuite," *Kansai Daigaku Tōzai gakujutsu kenkyūsho kiyō* 5 (1972).

The problems that Tokugawa Confucianists faced in their

appropriation of China are discussed by Kate Wildman Nakai in "The Naturalization of Confucianism in Tokugawa Japan: The Problem of Sinocentrism," *Harvard Journal of Asiatic Studies* 40 (June 1980), and *Shogunal Politics: Arai Hakuseki and the Premises of Tokugawa Rule* (Cambridge: Harvard University Press, 1988). Harry Harootunian adds to this in "The Functions of China in Tokugawa Thought," in Akira Iriye, ed., *The Chinese and the Japanese: Essays in Political and Cultural Interactions* (Princeton: Princeton University Press, 1980).

The impact of China's defeat in the Opium War has been studied by Ōba Osamu, above, and Haga Noboru, "Chūgoku to teikokushugi: Ahen sensō, Taihei tengoku, Nihon," in *Chūgoku kindaishi no shomondai—Tanaka Masayoshi Sensesi kinen rombunshū* (Tokyo, 1984); Ichiko Chūzō, "Bakumatsu Nihonjin no Taihei tengoku ni kansuru chishiki," in Motono Takeo, ed., *Meiji bunkashi ronshū* (Tokyo, 1952); and Etō Shinkichi, "Nihonjin no Chūgokukan—Takasugi Shinsaku ra no baai," in *Nihon to Ajiya—Niida Noboru Hakushi tsuitō rombunshū* (Tokyo, 1970).

My first book, *The Japanese and Sun Yat-sen* (Cambridge: Harvard University Press, 1954), took up the work of Asianists like Miyazaki Tōten, whose autobiography, translated and annoted by Etō Shinkichi and myself, appeared later as *My Thirty-Three Years' Dream: The Autobiography of Miyazaki Tōten* (Princeton: Princeton University Press, 1982). A more general discussion, "Japanese Views of China During the Meiji Period," appeared in Albert Feuerwerker, Rhoads Murphey, and Mary C. Wright, eds., *Approaches to Modern Chinese History* (Berkeley: University of California Press, 1967). My *Japan and China: From War to Peace, 1894–1972* (Chicago: Rand McNally, 1975) took up these themes again in a broader context.

Joshua Fogel has been particularly active in pursuing

themes of Meiji Sino-Japanese relations. His *Politics and Sinology: The Case of Naitō Konan, 1866–1934* (Cambridge: Harvard University Press) appeared in 1984, and a work is now in progress on travel diaries of Japanese visitors to China. Mention must also be made of Tam Yue-him of the Chinese University of Hong Kong, whose "An Intellectual's Response to Western Intrusion: Naitō Konan's View of Republican China," in Iriye, ed., *The Chinese and the Japanese*, promises a longer work. The dimensions of Sino-Japanese relations are so numerous, so interesting, and so important that one can expect the field to grow in size and depth.

Index

Haga Noboru, 101, 102n
Haga Yaichi, 4n
Hai-kuo t'u-chih, 74
Hall, Ivan Parker, 115n
Hall, John W., 28n
Hardacre, Helen, 95n
Harootunian, Harry, 83
Hatamoto ranks, 9
Hayashi Razan, 22
Hayashi Shihei, 88
Hayashiya Tatsuburō, 22n
Henderson, Dan Fenno, 65, 67n, 70n
Hideyoshi: conquest of Kyushu by, 8;
  invasion of Korea by, 17–18; trade
  permits under, 18
Hirado, 25–26
Hirata Atsutane, 82, 83, 90
"Hired foreigners," 55
Ho Ju-chang, 81
Hoshō system, 19, 22
Hosoi Heishū, 63, 68–69
Hosokawa Shigekata, 65
Hsiang-yüeh, 68
Hsiao Kung-chuan, 68

Ichiko Chūzō, 102n
Idemitsu Sazō, 113
I Fu-chiu, 60, 63–64
Ihara Saikaku, 40n
Ike no Taiga, 61, 63
"Imperial Confucianism," 68
Imperialism, during Meiji period,
  95–96
Imperial Military Exploits, 75
Imperial Rescript on Education, 69
Indo-China, French victory in, 105
Ingen, 55
Innes, Robert, 19n, 22n, 25n, 31n,
  35, 39
Inoue Kaoru, 106, 111, 115
Interpreters, Chinese, 13–14
Iquan, Nicholas (Cheng Chih-lung),
  26–27
Irokawa Daikichi, 81, 84, 93
Itakura Katsushige, 22

Itō Hirobumi, 114
Itowappu, 18, 30
Iwakura embassy, 95
Iwao Seiichi, 9, 14n, 17, 19n, 21, 23n

Janes, L. L., 64
Japan: isolation of, 2; Chinese artisans
  in, 7–8; centralist view of, 79–80,
  82; military prowess of, 84, 85; as
  national entity, 86–87; political and
  trade activity of, 93; as bound to fate
  of China, 101; as European-style empire, 106–107; war with Russia, 112
Japan-centered world order, 2
Japanese Confucianists, 83, 107–110;
  problems faced by, 77–78
Japanese governance, extension of,
  95–96
Japanese law codes, 66
Japanese superiority, views of, 79, 84,
  94; during Meiji period, 95
Jih-pen i-chien, 7
Jiyū-minken (People's Rights), 103
Jōkyō era regulations, 29

Kaibōsaku, 90
Kaigo Tokiomi, 69n
Kaikoku heidan, 88
Kaisho, 31
Kamiya Nobuyuki, 14
Kanō school of artists, 80
Kanshi, 80–81
Katō Eiichi, 17
Katō Kiyomasa, 9
Katsu Kaishū, 97
Katsura Tarō, 103
Kawamura Ichio, 108n
Kawashima Motojirō, 22n
Keene, Donald, 81n, 85n
Ketelaar, James Edward, 95n
Ketōjin, 87
Ki Baitei, 61
Kido Takayoshi, 62, 102
Kimura Tadashi, 116n
Kobata Atsushi, 16, 29